Keep It Together Man

For Dads with a
Special Kid

By Rick Daynes

copyright ©2016 Rick Daynes 2nd Edition

info@keepittogetherman.org

Published by: Showme Publishing,

14520 Camino de la Luna No. 2

San Diego, CA 92127

Cover Art: Bryan Niven contact@bryanniven.com

Graphic Work: Shaun Miner: shaun@greenroomleads.com

Editing/Book Layout: Janie Van Komen: janievankomen.com

ISBN: 978-0-9974624-0-1

This book is dedicated to:
Every parent
who has had that moment
when they thought
they knew what they were doing,
only to find out
they didn't know jack squat.

Keep It Together Man

For Dads With a Special Kid

TABLE OF CONTENTS

Part III Happy Wife Happy Life

The Club

End Notes

Introduction:

The Luckiest Man on Earth

2012 was perhaps the best year so far in the Daynes family home. Halfway through the year, my wife, Robin, turned 36-years-old and was in the best shape of her life. That's saying a lot since she was a division I college tennis player, among other things. We were able to get away for not one, but two POG's (Parents Only Getaway). Our kids were doing relatively well and it seemed like problems were a thing of the past. Peace and calm reigned in our once turbulent home.

After a lot of prayer, we felt there was one more child for us to bring into the world. Plus, we had this unbelievably adorable two-year-old little girl who was such a delight! If ever I had a bad day, all I had to do was close my eyes and think of our little princess and everything seemed to be OK. My wife said, "If you can guarantee it's a girl, we will have one more." And so I did what any man would do. I stepped up to the plate and guaranteed it.

This was quite a stretch since I don't make a lot of money and we live in small quarters where things are cramped as it is. Plus, we had two boys in special education that required a lot of attention. Both of them however had overcome so much in the past few years. At the moment they were doing fantastic. We figured out a way to make one more child fit in the mix, and were anxious to put our plan into action.

Our second POG of the year took us to our old stomping grounds in Key West Florida, followed by an Eastern Caribbean cruise. We returned home tan, rested, pregnant, and ready to take on the world. As the pregnancy progressed, we made plans for the birth of our second beautiful little princess with blue eyes and tight blond curls. I was sure of it. Bring on that little angel!

Further along in her pregnancy, Robin decided to take a blood test to determine if there was a chance of any kind of chromosomal abnormalities. She had never taken the test before. But apparently once you hit 35 years old, your risk dramatically increases to one in 308. Big deal! She became pregnant less than three months after her 36th birthday. There is a better chance of falling down on the ground and dying than our baby having any kind of chromosome issue.[1] The results came back low on alpha-feta protein. This moved us way up to a one in 20 chance of having a child with Down Syndrome. I realize that's a pretty good jump. But still, one in 20! That's nothing! A long shot at best.

A few days later we went to see the perinatologist for further testing. The first thing they did was an ultra sound and found two things of concern. First and most obvious, she moved the lens into a position as if the baby was sitting on the camera. And there, much to my dismay was the obvious site of the kid's donger. Ugh. It's a boy. I couldn't believe it. Gone was the princess. Gone was the sweetness. Gone was the guarantee! I threw my arms against the wall and braced myself before apologizing to my wife.

Everything else looked normal until they came to the baby's heart where there was a very small white speck. The perinatologist explained to us that the speck just doubled our chances of Down Syndrome. At this point they used to do an amniocentesis to determine Trisomy 21 (Down Syndrome). However, thanks to modern medicine, the mother can now take a blood test. So we said no thanks to sticking a large needle into my wife's belly dangerously close to our baby, and opted for the blood test.

We went in to that doctor's office with a one in 20 chance and walked out with a one in 10 chance. Still, one in 10. That's nothing! One in 10! I'll take those odds any day. That's a 90% chance our baby is totally normal. And of course he's normal! We're healthy! We're in shape! We have great genes! One of my grandfathers died unexpectedly at 94 years old, the other at 101! We have no physical problems on either side of the family. My mother-in-law delivered a healthy baby at age 46! You're telling me that her daughter, who is 10 years younger, is at any kind of risk? Our baby is part of the healthy 90% for sure. It's a done deal.

A week later I called Robin's obstetrician. I've never made a move like this before. But I was concerned as this pregnancy had been a killer! Just a few months ago, Robin was at a 5:30AM exercise class six days a week. She was juggling kids, sports, church, extracurricular activities of all kinds, and did I mention... working part time as a Registered Nurse? When was the last time you did a 12 hour shift, on your feet, running around taking care of sick people all day? Oh my mistake, when was the last time you did all that from 7PM to 7AM? My mother says Robin is the most driven person she knows. She is fantastic if I do say so myself.

And yet, this pregnancy had reduced her to a shell of her former self. She struggled to get out of bed at any mid-morning hour. She was in a constant battle between her will and her ever-changing body. She had been pregnant before of course, but nothing like this. This was torture. This was a physical, emotional, mental thrashing. And she was not going to try to get any help. She was going to tell herself to suck it up and get going. Then there was weeping and wailing and gnashing of teeth followed by my putting her to bed and telling her to stay there, I got this. That was followed by a lot of sleep, then guilt, and then, repeat the process.

So I called her Obstetrician, because that's what I do. The doctor was at the hospital, so I spoke to the nurse who would relay information back and forth from me to the OB. I asked if there was any way to get the blood test results as that would surely help Robin feel better. At one point, the nurse called me and said the doctor would like to see Robin at the hospital. Apparently, the doctor has some time to address Robin's health issues.

Rick: (feeling uneasy) Are the test results in?

Nurse: Yes, the doctor has them and can discuss them with you when you go to the hospital.

Rick: (dark cloud enshrouds) What are the results?

Nurse: I cannot give out test results.

Rick: (reality sinks in) It's positive isn't it.

Nurse: (deafening silence)

Rick: That's OK; you don't need to say anything.

Nurse: (choked up) I'm sorry.

The next 10 minutes I spent on my knees. And then I went into our bedroom where my wife was lying in bed, sick from this pregnancy. Despite my best efforts to be strong, she could tell I was shaken. She sat up in bed, I pulled a chair up and we held hands for a moment. I said whatever I could to give her love and strength and then told her our baby had Down Syndrome.

Since that stormy moment, there has been a lot of darkness. Breakdowns are at times frequent and questions unanswered. We had the amniocenteses, which confirmed the blood test result, and crying became more common. It hasn't been all bad though. In fact, my sweetheart and I have bonded and become stronger in our commitment and love to each other. In fact, the day I wrote this was Valentine's Day. I had to work in another city and so we were not together. But I was looking at a card she sent with me. I could not open it. Every time I looked at it, I cried like a baby. There was a power emitting from that red envelope and I knew what it said. It would be full of love and humility and gentleness from a woman battling every day.

At that moment, I knew that she loved me more than anything on earth. And she knows the same holds true from me to her. Since the week our diagnosis was confirmed, we have become stronger and stronger. Sometimes trials will do that. And sometimes they will do the opposite.

I hope you will find value in these experiences and sound results internalizing these principles. If you apply them, they will, without a doubt, bring a peace and happiness to a level you have never imagined. I am a living testament of that. I have one princess and four beautiful boys, one with Autism, one with Aspergers, and one with Down syndrome. And I am the luckiest man on the face of the earth.

Acknowledgment

Dear Robin,

When Tyler started to make real progress and our burdens of raising a family with a special needs child were lightened, all I could
think about was finally getting in a surf. While I was thinking
about hitting the waves, you asked me, "What are we going to do to
help others?"

I just completed my book. I hope it will help some family the way
we have been helped. As I reflect on those selfless people and organizations who help us weather the storms with their time, talents,
examples, programs, literature, encouragement, and resources, I
am in humble admiration.

As much as I hope this work helps others, I must admit I wrote
it in most part for me. We are never out of the woods with any of
our children, and I need this script for guidance in dealing with
our children and you. Sometimes I forget that we think differently.
We act differently, have our own ideas, and are by nature, different. There are times when these differences collide in explosions
we have trouble recovering from. Ultimately, we learn to accept
each other. We will mend our bond, and unite as the leaders of our
special family.

You will not like some things I wrote in this book. I wrote it from
my perspective, "A man, wondering what the heck happened to
my life and my wife?" After much research, it turns out that my
struggles are no different than that of my fellow testosterone in-
fested friends. Although, we men don't like to discuss, dissect, and
express our afflictions and feelings, for the sake of this book, I have
swallowed my pride and done my best to convey some thoughts
and encouragement. It might help a brother out.

You'll be offended and wonder what your friends think. I already know what my friends think. I'll be receiving panty hose and various feminine products for several birthdays down the road. After what we've been through, we are so beyond caring what outside onlookers think. May I please publish this and share?

Love,

Rick

Black Friday

Beep beep, beep beep, beep beep.

Oh please no. It can't possibly be 3:30 yet. I just went to sleep. My foggy vision checks the alarm clock for the unsightful confirmation of 3:30AM. Muscles ache, bones quake, oh my back is going to break, as I wrestle the comforter off my battered body.

Curse that Turkey Bowl! That once a year event where we come out of athletic retirement, and pretend we're 18 again. That glorious tradition of football followed by feast, passed down from generation to generation, designed to inflict pain and punishment on the weekend warrior, or rather the yearly warrior.

Every fiber in my body aches as the icy air penetrates my So Cal winter clothes. Perhaps another sweatshirt could have done me some good, I thought as I shifted into drive and headed on my way. No matter, I was determined to be the good husband and go the extra mile for my beautiful wife who had given me the holiday assignment.

My mission was an easy one. Department store opens for the big after Thanksgiving Day sale at 4:00AM. Simply purchase two portable DVD players on sale today to the first customers through the door. Make sure you use the first coupon for the additional 20% discount (limit five per person) and pay for it with the department store credit card, thus giving us an additional 10% off. Upon checkout, make sure I receive an additional $30 mail in rebate coupon for each DVD player. Make sure the total is more than $60 to get an additional $10 store credit to be used at a later time.

The first time my wife had given me those instructions, it was as if she were speaking some sort of ancient long forgotten language.

I had fumbled the ball on my wife's instructions before, so I knew what to do. Rehearse, practice, rehearse again, cheat sheet, everything written down, rehearse again.

It was 3:36AM and no one was on the streets. I was in the zone and flying. I'll be there 15 minutes before it opens and probably the first in line, I thought to myself. I'll execute the mission and back in my warm bed by 4:30AM easy. Oh yes, I would return victorious with DVD players in hand! I could see the look on my children's faces as they opened up their Christmas presents. I could feel the warm hug from my wife knowing that every family trip from now on would be a family film festival on wheels. Oh the peace of absent sibling fights in cramped quarters! The happiness! And I would be the hero! Two minutes ahead of schedule I pulled into the parking lot brimming with confidence.

Ohhhhh! oh no, no noooooo! No way on earth is this happening! My brimming confidence was shattered as I viewed the over-ripe parking lot. Where on earth did all these people come from? It's 3:43 in the morning for crying out loud! A black cloud enshrouds my hopes and dreams of a happy Christmas. Perhaps this is why they call it Black Friday?

Rick focus! All is not lost! Though that parking space is lost, and now that one, and yep I'm getting snaked again. My foot becomes heavy as I race towards the final stall in the row. I am Lightning McQueen unlawfully speeding to victory! But wait, from the other direction, here comes Chick vying for the same last spot. The foot becomes heavier as Lightning accelerates through the turn and takes the Piston Cup!

Like a cat from its cage I sprang from the car. But like a dog that's run out of leash I am jerked to the reality of my aching legs. Curse that Turkey Bowl! My stride reduces to a limp and I hop-scurry to the entrance.

Oh the horror! Is that the line? You gotta be kidding me! These people are all psychos! With adrenaline rushing, I quicken my pace and lengthen my stride in search of the end of the line. I follow the line along the storefront to the end of the property. Then a right turn leads me along the outer parameter of the parking lot. I stare

13

into the black of the foggy pre-dawn hour in search of the end. Perhaps this is why they call it Black Friday? You've got to get up in the black of the night to get a good deal.

Lit by the streetlights of the back of the parking lot, I discover the end of the line. "This is crazy," I announce to my fellow runners who have made the same mistake I have. To which came the reply, "Must be your first time, eh?" The voice came from one of three suburban soccer moms passing me on the right. This is not happening! I down shift, hit the gas, ignore the unrelenting throb of strained muscles, and race past the shopping sprinters to the rapidly growing line.

I'm hit! Like an electric shock, pain stretches through my body as I grip my pulled hamstring. Reduced again to a limp, I hop along as I'm passed by the soccer moms and everyone else rushing to the end of the line. The spirit is willing, but the flesh is weak, and I stagger to the final resting stop and claim my spot at the end of the line. Totally dejected I lean against a car to catch my breath and gather myself.

The phrase 'adding insult to injury' becomes my reality as I gaze upon my own car. I can see it almost spitting distance away. I just ran a giant circle! I wanted to spit, I was so mad! But my mouth was dry as the desert and my lungs were burning. The spit would have turned to ice and cracked the front windshield knowing my luck. Twelve minutes 'til the doors open. If one-tenth of the crowd in front of me goes for the DVD players, I will return home in shame.

The clock struck 4:00AM and off the jumbled pack of shoppers, including me, went. The anticipation leading to this moment was almost too much to bear. As they herded the cattle into the arena I rehearsed my game plan again and again. Just get in, swallow your pride and ask for directions. The doors grew closer. The sounds of commotion coming from inside the great and spacious building echo in my ears. I can almost smell the DVD players now! Hey, am I the only man in this line?

I was so far out of my element! And I knew it! I entered the department store and chaos ensued. Where are the DVD players? I shouted over the crowd. I did have a height advantage, but that was all I had going for myself. For these were competitors I had never faced before, and THEY KNEW IT! Where are the DVD players? DVD players? Portable DVD players? An employee standing on a chair attempting to keep some kind of order pointed me across the bustling market. I had my heading.

Still nursing my hamstring I darted through traffic toward the prize. I quickly came to an impediment; a large pyramid of something was being mobbed by a crowd 5 people deep. What is it? I shouted! But no one answered. Yet boxes of something were leaving the stack at an alarming rate. I turned sideways, raised my arms in the air, and squeezed my way toward the goodies. "Is this the DVD player?" I asked a lady next to me. "I don't know," came her reply. "Then why are you trying to get one?" I asked. Her answer surprised me, "Because everyone else wants one!"

It was as if blood was in the water and these sharks were out to get some. Some of what? I didn't know if anyone on the outside knew, but the feeding frenzy was in full swing and I was now one of the predators. I grabbed a box. It wasn't what I had hoped for, and again I set off in the same direction.

At this point I surveyed the area. There were several groups similar to the one I had just encountered. People seem to be mobbing sporadic items throughout the store. Ouch, what was that? Did I just get an elbow to the ribs? I thought, OH, IT IS ON! LADY!

I then circled the next mob of shoppers attacking another pyramid of boxes. It probably wasn't the DVD player, but I didn't care. My attitude had turned to KICK BUTT NOW! Ask questions later! If it's something I don't want, I'll discard it before checkout. But for now, I've got to have whatever everyone else is getting. I waited a second longer and ambushed my prey.

I now had two boxes and was on to my third. And then I saw it. At first I thought it was a mistake, but it wasn't. There in the front row of the next mosh pit, was a man. I was on the perimeter of the circle and yelled, "Dude!" He looked at me with a war torn look in his eyes. He could see the same in my eyes, and we instantly bonded. He wasn't going anywhere. The mosh pit around him was 7 to

10 women deep and had pinned him in. He didn't say a word, but grabbed a box from the coveted shelf and threw it to me. I pointed at him as if to say, "You're the man." His facial expression was clear. Take what you can and save yourself. Three boxes were now in hand, none of which was what I wanted. I left my new brother drowning in the sea of grabbers and pressed on.

Taking more elbows to the mid section, I navigated through the aggressive thicket. Onward! I was getting close. I could feel it. I shouted to anyone who would listen, "Portable DVD players?" "Portable DVD Players!" Finally an answer came from a worker taking refuge behind a partition. "If there are any left, they should be over there." I pivoted and ran to the scarcely populated shelves.

My eyes ran through the shelves. They were nowhere to be found. All was lost. I would return home in shame. Then came a distinctly low voice from the other side of the isle. It was the first male voice I had heard yet that day. He said to me, "If you're looking for the portable DVD players, they're right here." I sprinted to the spot and discovered a large area of empty shelves picked over by the masses. THERE WERE FIVE DVD PLAYERS LEFT. All five were stacked on the top shelf one on top of the other, five high. He had stacked them, and was about to lift all five and head to the cashier. I remember seeing the ad, "Limit 5 per person." He asked me how many I needed. I gave him the peace sign and he took off with three boxes, leaving me the last two. Still holding my fingers in V-formation, I realized VICTORY WAS MINE!

Following a successful check-out experience in which I executed my wife's directions with exactness, I savored the victory all the way until my grinning face hit my down pillow. The plan was successful and sweet was my triumph. It could not have come at a better time. My life, at this time, was void of plans and empty of victories.

My kindergartener's daily schooling experience consisted of meeting in a closet-like classroom, all by himself with a full-time aide, and, almost always, some kind of specialist. He was placed there after several incidences of bad behavior from hitting teachers to running away from school. We had been offered NPS (Non Public School), which means the district will pay for his education elsewhere, because they just can't handle him. I'll get into our story later, but I was living in an environment much like that department store on Black Friday.

Every day I was out of my element rushing through the crowd, trying to keep pace. I was trying to execute my plan, or lack thereof, while taking several metaphoric shots to the ribs. Heck, I was just trying to survive! Like that department store, I could not understand the voraciousness of my new world. It was so unfamiliar and volatile to me. The smallest thing would induce overly emotional reactions. I was living on unstable ground, just waiting for something to break loose. Constantly looking for a helping hand, I needed directions before it was too late. Before the portable DVD players are all gone! WHERE ARE THE DVD PLAYERS!? Where is rationality, organization, happiness and peace?

There was peace at our last IEP meeting. Well, she was there for roll call anyway, but ducked out at the first hint of hostility. Peace had a better place to be, and left me empty to fend for myself. I put more preparation into that meeting than I did into Black Friday. Rehearse, practice, rehearse again, cheat sheet, write everything down, rehearse again. There were 14 people in attendance for that four-hour meeting, including the Principal, the Special Education Director, teachers, psychologists, and attorneys. Again, I was the only male in the room.

On that shoppers' Black Friday morning, I only remember seeing a small handful of men among hundreds of women. A couple of men were dropping off women and then hunkering down in their cars while the women went in for the fight.

One man was immersed against the pyramid of what I was hoping was the portable DVD players. A hundred women in that mosh pit, and yet he heard me give the universal male distress signal, "Dude!" He saw me in the back of the pack trying to get in, when he was trying to get out. Neither one of us was going anywhere. He took one look at my face and he knew I was out of my element. He knew I did not belong and that I didn't want to be there! He took the coveted box from the pyramid. And he chucked it off his back foot like a quarterback going down. Over the out stretched arms of

17

the defenders to my grateful hands came the package. I was so appreciative, and he knew it.

In the war of the store, I finally reached my proper destination only to find it had been totally ravaged. It was like a swarm of fire ants had come through and picked the bone clean. Nothing but empty shelves was all I could see. I groaned in frustration as I was done. Then a deep voice came from the other side of the shelves. "If you're looking for the portable DVD players, they're over here." Quickly, I ran around the shelves to his isle. And there, on the shelf were five DVD players all stacked on top of each other with this guy guarding it.

He had grabbed five when the rush was on and took them to the safe house where he could regroup. He had the power to send me home empty handed, dejected, with my tail between my legs. He was certainly on his way out the door with those five boxes. Like the guy stuck in the mosh pit, he knew my story. I was there solely at the behest of my wife, and he knew it. He could tell I had never done this before, that I had no idea where to go and what to do. Had you asked him, he probably would have told you I had a limp because of the Turkey Bowl just 18 hours previous!

Wingman

If you have a child with special needs of any kind, like those two guys in the department store that Black Friday morning, I see the look in your eyes. Perhaps I understand a little of what you're going through or about to go through. I've been there before and I'm still there. Believe me, I get it. And I've got your back.

I have no academic training to counsel people. No psych degree here I'm afraid. In the first psychology class I took in college, the teacher began by saying most psych majors are in it to figure out what's wrong with themselves. It was the best opening line ever from a teacher. A lot of the shrinks and professional experts have good things to say. I've listened to them, read their books and studied their lessons. I've taken their classes, training, "Things" (more about that later), and step-by-step programs. This book is not that.

If I had to do it over again, I'd hit Black Friday totally differently. I'd send one guy there hours earlier, maybe even camp out, depending on the stakes. I'd bring the minivan/assault vehicle with a few guys I forced out of bed with some kind of bribe. I'd arm them with two-way radios and a well-rehearsed offensive game plan. I would send one guy on a down and out to the X Boxes, another on a post corner to the flat screen TV's, and my fastest receiver on a deep fade to the corner of the end zone where he could score the portable DVD players.

And if I had to raise another special needs child, which I am doing, I will go about it very differently. I will cut out the fat and curve the programs, focusing only on what's most important. There is way too much time, energy and money spent on projects not worth their billing.

I passed two more men as I was on my way out of the store Black-Friday morning. They were slack jawed, heads down, arms resting to their sides, and empty handed. Their eyes had long passed deer in the headlights and were now glazed over with failure. That was my plight just moments earlier. DON'T BE THAT GUY! Don't get caught in the chaos, 'clueless.' Let me give you a heads up. I am now that guy who chucked that package. I'm that guy who passed out the last DVD player on the shelf to a brother who had taken his licks. Take the box. Read it, apply it, and live. Most of all "Keep It Together, Man."

Peace out,

Wingman

Part I
Perspective and Pursuit

Tyler's Year

"When everything seems to be going against you, remember that the airplane takes off against the wind, not with it." Henry Ford

We have benefitted immensely from books written about special needs kids, programs, doctors, teachers, administrators, and other parents. I have learned some valuable lessons. I wish someone would have taken me aside when this was just beginning and given me a heads up of what was to come and how to handle it. I am still in this battle and perhaps will be for the rest of my life. But things are a whole lot better around my house because of learning from others.

Our efforts to achieve happiness or glimpses of it during our worst struggles were often aided by reading stories of other families in like circumstances. It was comforting to know we were not alone. Before I get to the do's and don'ts, and as tough as it is to capture the day to day grind in a few pages, this, in a nutshell is part of our story.

My wife Robin and I started having children when we lived in Key West Florida. Three days following the fateful attacks of 9/11/2001 our little Conch was born at Key West Hospital. Jefferson, was as precocious a child as I had ever seen. There was not one aspect of childhood he wasn't early to learn and develop. Physically, socially, academically, he was well beyond kids his age. We started him a year early in school and could have started him two years early.

Twenty-five months after Jefferson was born, and 3 ½ weeks before his due date, our second son, Tyler, was born into our family in San Diego, California. He was a happy healthy baby whom we absolutely adored. He was beautiful, and we loved watching him grow along with his older brother. It was clear early on that he was not going to excel as his older brother had. Because we had an advanced child first, it was difficult to measure the progress of our second. Every time we'd think something might be wrong with him, someone would say something to the effect that he's totally normal, it's just that his older brother is off the charts.

Preschool

Preschool was a three-hour everyday event that seemed to throw up more and more red flags. He became defiant in his behavior. Often upset, he was difficult to teach and direct into tasks and activities. My wife, Robin, was surprised one day when she observed Tyler in his classroom. For the most part, he didn't participate with his class. He was disruptive and had his own timeout area. This served no purpose as he wouldn't go there when asked anyway. He became a "runner," fleeing the classroom randomly. Robin began working closely with the teacher and her aides and nothing seemed to work.

Towards the end of preschool, we called the district and asked for him to be evaluated. They could not do it at that time because the calendar was booked until the end of the school year. Nevertheless we enlisted the help of the Kindergarten Special Education Teacher and others for help.

PEPP (Poway's Extended Primary Program)

We were fortunate to have a program in our school district called PEPP (Poway's Extended Primary Program). This program is designed for kids who are not quite ready for kindergarten. We were very excited for PEPP as it came with a great teacher we were sure would turn our boy around. She was a seasoned teacher who had raised four boys of her own. We had several friends who had their children go through her class, and all raved. She'll know what to do. She'll get him on track. My wife took Ty to school a couple of days early to introduce him to the teacher and new classroom. We set up everything we could think of for his best possible chance of success.

Two weeks later he was by himself sitting at his own horseshoe table in the back of the class. He had his own projects and activities to engage him that sometimes worked. Once again, he would not participate with the class. As soon as the teacher gave an inch on anything, Tyler took a mile. Three weeks into the year, Ty was running out of class and exhibiting all the behaviors of Preschool.

IEP (Individualized Education Plan)

Hiding under his desk, a couple noteworthy tantrums, and one biting the teacher on the inner thigh--hastened the district's evaluation timeline and our IAT (Intervention Assistance Team) meetings. We had our first official meeting with the teacher, school psychologist, principal, and others. We discussed getting him an aide, timeline, and corrective actions we could take. The team was helpful with the exception of one person, the Principal. It's kind of an important person on the team.

She was new, inexperienced, and clearly had no business being a Principal. At one point, she got frustrated and blurted out, "You know he's four! He doesn't need to be in school!" This was the first, but not the last that I would grapple to hold my tongue in one of these meetings. She just wanted the problem to go away, and taking our boy out of her school was the easiest solution. Even though we were new at this, it was obvious that all members of what would become our IEP team would be crucial. The Principal, of course, is not a good one to have a riff with.

Following the meeting, a member of the team hinted to us in confidence that we needed to be prepared for a long and arduous journey. I remember thinking, what on earth are we getting ourselves into? How many people like this Principal would we have to deal with? Will this team really have our son's best interest at heart? I was beginning to feel emotions I had never felt before. I just wanted this to be as painless as possible for my son and wife. I wanted people to love my boy and help him succeed.

It was becoming increasingly clear, that although I was sure most people in this profession are where they are because they genuinely like or even love what they do, there would always be that bad apple. One or two people on the team could make our lives troublesome. For a parent just beginning this process, the fear of uncertainty was already the culprit of many sleepless nights.

Shortly after our meeting, Tyler was officially evaluated by the district and our first IEP meeting was on the horizon. Day after day we pushed to hurry the evaluation along. By law, they have to finish the evaluation within 90 days. What I don't understand is why they seem to always take the entire 90 days? Dealing with our boy and the daily complications he brought, made 90 days feel like 90 weeks.

Preparing for our first IEP meeting was no small task. I drove 45 minutes to an office where I met with an IEP Specialist who trained me in the fine art of the IEP meeting. First thing she did was hand me a book as thick as the Bible and tell me I needed to read and know it. It contains all the current laws and regulations. And good news! A new edition comes out every year! Can't wait for next year's addition! Yeah! Not really. Then we talked about what to do. What to say. What's it like. Who is there. Who speaks. Who conducts. What to bring. Whether or not we need an advocate. What to wear. How to act. When to sign forms. Who will help us review. And on and on and on.

We walked into that meeting with pad and paper, a basket of food and drinks, manuals and notes in hand, digital recorders poised, and back-ups for everything.

Diagnosis

"A person's a person, no matter how small. "
Dr. Seuss

Six months or so previous to our first IEP meeting began the run of
the doctors. Robin took Tyler to his primary pediatrician who told
us our son was ADHD and wrote him a prescription for Ritalin.
We had Kaiser Insurance, and took Ty to the "Learning Center,"
where they tested him and put him through exercises and continued evaluations. They said he has an over the top imagination and
blew us off. Robin took Tyler to Occupational therapy every week.
We became more aware of his sensory needs. I began to understand why things were always too loud for him and why he was
like a bull in a china shop. We always thought he was so clumsy
but yet exhibited amazing balance at times. We discovered that
he enjoyed sensory input from crashing into things. He would look
at himself in the mirror for long periods of time, watching himself
move in various ways. We were beginning to understand him and
developed a sensory plan and diet.

Robin then took Ty to a psychologist who was an expert in the field
of childhood learning disorders. He spent less than 20 minutes
with him and he told us he was absolutely Bipolar. He was visibly
uncomfortable with the way Tyler behaved. He said he could not
help us unless he was medicated and asked us to see a psychiatrist
for a prescription. Some things we were smart enough to decide
early on, such as medication. We knew medication played a big
part in the lives of many kids like our son. We did not have all the
facts but decided to keep an open mind even though the initial
thought of medicating our son made us sick.

We decided to address medication only after all other options had
failed. So we said good bye to our first psychologist and everyone
else who wanted to start therapy with medication. We saw a psychiatrist and Tyler hid under the chairs while we talked. Ty wore
one of his superhero costumes he loves so much. After an hour the
psychiatrist gave us a laundry list of possible diagnoses. He want-

26

ed to give us a prescription for Risperdal. Luckily Robin is a registered nurse and familiar with some of these drugs. She explained to me that Risperdal is an anti psychotic drug. I thought, this doctor spent an hour with Tyler. He couldn't give us any viable answers, but wanted to put our four-year-old boy on anti-psychotic medication? We declined. Then on to another psychologist, then a psychiatrist, and so on.

Robin was absolute in her resolve to figure out what was wrong with our boy and was taking him anywhere and everywhere she could to get help. Tyler was four years old turning five shortly and we desperately wanted to uncover who he really was. We wanted to know who he was supposed to grow up to be without muddying his mind and body with unnecessary medication, labels, or programs. Doctors gave us all kinds of possibilities from Oppositional Defiant Disorder to Aspergers to Autism. All diagnoses came with its own set of programs. This is what he has, and this is who he'll be for the rest of his life, and here's how to deal with it, came the echo from the experts. The specialists were all over the map. Some were confidant in their diagnosis and others vague. Many of their opinions were contrary to each other. I learned that there are good people willing to help, others who just want your money, medications are easy to come by, and real answers can be impossible to find. Whereas we began with such hope, these doctors really brought about a loss of faith and trust in them.

By the time our school district evaluated Tyler, he had already had every diagnosis thrown at him, but nothing definitive for us to accept. We didn't stick with anyone long enough to get an official diagnosis because most wanted to medicate him. At this point, I really did not care what label they slapped on him as long as he qualified for Special Education and got the help he needed. The diagnosis from the district was read by the school Psychologist along with a lengthy list of official jargon. The declaration of the primary diagnosis was, "Autism," with a secondary diagnosis of, "Other health impaired."

The Road to Recovery

And thus began our journey into Special Education. At our next meeting we discovered our immature Principal had been dismissed from the school and replaced by a gentleman who came out of retirement at the request of the district. What a difference one person can make! The team decided to keep Tyler in his current PEPP (Poway's Extended Primary Program) classroom and give him an aide. We had actually asked for this before, but because of budget cuts, we had no success. People on our IEP team hinted that it was the result of the new principal, who took it upon himself to get involved in our son's case. We thanked him openly and he looked at us and said, "It's what he needs."

Ty was given a young man as his aide, still in college, with little to no experience as an aide. The school psychologist trained him as he worked with Tyler and actually did quite well. He also had a resource pull out in a smaller classroom with the psychologist, circle of friends, occupational therapy, and speech therapy. Every day was still stressful, wondering what events or setbacks would happen. But we were very happy with his aide and the work of the team in helping Tyler learn and grow.

Summer School

Our end of school IEP meeting was a celebration of sorts. A child was in need. The need was addressed and met. It was really a successful effort for everyone involved. We patted each other on the back and grazed on fruit and sweets. We talked about his growth since his diagnosis and the progress he had made. Smiles were everywhere as we thanked the team for their efforts and friendship to our family. The only thing wrong with the meeting was that there were only two members of the team in attendance. Nevertheless, we had such a wonderful team and experience that we couldn't imagine anything but the best success for our boy.

Still all smiles, we debated his future placement. We discussed all the options on the table and decided to take the advice of our Program Specialist and place him in a Special Day Class for summer that would be taught half of the time by the district's Autism Specialist. We had some experience with her and really liked that placement. As for the class beginning the next school year, there was a lot of uncertainty regarding what was available for ASD (Autism Spectrum Disorder) classes, which was what the team decided was best for Tyler. The Summer school class would stay together for the Fall school year, but there was not room enough for Ty to continue with them.

Frustrated that we were not given any choices in his placement, we were uncomfortable with the idea of beginning next year in a class we didn't know anything about. There was talk of a new ASD class that would form at a new school. We probed, and heard rumors of a new teacher and then possibly a seasoned teacher. We were skeptical taking the recommendation from the school district. Was it too much to ask to know who the teacher would be and where it was? Would it be the least restrictive environment for him? It was difficult putting our son in the hands of our team, which was really driven by our Program Specialist, but what choice did we have? The anxiety of going into the next school year blindly was buffered by the fact that we had ended on such a positive note. Really what could go wrong?

The Year In Hell

"If you're going through Hell, keep going."
Winston Churchill

Following a successful six-week ASD (Autism Spectrum Disorder) Summer School program, we geared up for the school year. Robin took Tyler to meet his new teacher, school, and classroom a few days before our opening day of Kindergarten. The program and class were new to the school and the teacher had a fresh degree and still taking classes, I believe, for her Masters.

Things started off okay for about a week. They began the day by mainstreaming Tyler with an aide for reading, a subject he detests. He began to protest and act out because he didn't want to read. If he acted out loud enough, he was rewarded by getting pulled

29

out of reading and back to his normal classroom. The idea of task avoidance was realized and snowballed into any subject or activity he did not want to do. It took little Tyler less than two weeks to realize that he could control his day at school, the teacher, and the class. A sudden reaction, unorthodox behavior, or an escalating tantrum brought with it all kinds of reactions from the teacher, aides, and faculty. In many ways, it was a game to him. And thus the games began.

One day, Robin had a meeting with Ty's teacher. Robin went out of her way to get to the meeting and then the teacher dodged Robin on campus. The principal came out and told Robin that the teacher couldn't meet with her. She was feeling overwhelmed or something and couldn't face my wife. Really? This is the best teacher for us? Our son's teacher was dropped off and picked up from school every day by her mother. And her mother participated in class events and brought food and treats. It was just awkward. This teacher was nowhere near the right teacher for my son.

Calls started to come home on a daily basis. Robin frequently had to pick him up during school. Before the month of September was up, we had had three IEP meetings to address his problematic situations. He had issues on the bus and occasionally with the bus driver. Sometimes he did not want to get off the bus altogether. What we thought was a simple task like getting him to come off the bus, was a monumental feat for his teacher. So Robin started driving him to school every day. The school was not close. She would play with him, see him to his line, and take him to his class where they would begin the day. But that did not help.

The time commitment was debilitating as every day brought more incidences. Robin was stretched to the limit and I picked up what she could not get done. Every day was a grind with no relief in sight. Another day Ty got angry and tipped over a very small plastic bookshelf. It had two shelves beginning at the floor and was thigh high at best and probably a little longer than it was tall. You could easily do a Captain Morgan stance on it. It had a dozen children's books on the shelf, and was placed in the middle of the room.

This was a perfect location to let everyone know that he was upset. So he easily tipped it over without anyone being close. The problem was made worse by the teacher, who I'm sure followed all proper safety procedures to the letter of the law and evacuated all students and aides out of the classroom.

We did our best working with the teacher, but our relationship with her was not any better than her relationship to our son. She was immature, inexperienced, and clearly in over her head. Our frustrations with her were building by the day as she continued to exhibit the inability to deal with our child. We brought in team members and outside helpers who had success with Tyler previously. They gave advice, but the teacher was selective and slow in what she'd implement in Tyler's program. The psychologist from the previous year told us, "All the things we had in place for him last year are gone."

He grabbed a toy rake on the playground and twirled it around like a martial arts character. His teacher feared for the safety of the other children and faculty and scurried everyone to the safety of the classrooms. I later explained to the teacher that he is five years old and likes to pretend he is a ninja warrior. He and his three year old brother play this together all the time. They twirl sticks and strike poses and pretend they have powers. That's what little boys do.

Now he knows he has powers because dozens of kids will run into their classrooms when he has a stick. Getting a stick out of Tyler's hand is not difficult. Ty's little brother does it daily. I'm pretty sure he could have talked Tyler off the bus as well. All this over-reaction empowered our boy and his actions regressed further. He began to have trouble with the speech teacher and occupational therapist. More calls were made home, more trips to school were made.

The downward spiral continued, and he learned about running away. Boy did that get a reaction! Nothing like a five year old running out of school and down the street. The principal picked him up in her van once and played a DVD for him. Ty must have made a mental note: Run away from school, and you get to watch a movie! So that happened again and again.

Every day brought a new incident, a new problem. Tyler hit an aide. Tyler kicked the teacher. Tyler ran out of school again and this time made it to a busy four-way intersection. The teacher told us it was against the law for her to follow him. Are you beginning to feel our frustration? What teacher in their right mind lets a five year old boy run out of school and down to a busy four-way inter-section? 7-Eleven was just beyond the other side of the intersec-tion. They called the police to go get him. Other times, the princi-pal would get him.

He loved the principal and would frequently run to her office. A couple times he ran, no one knew where he was. The principal sent the teacher home one day because she was dizzy. She couldn't handle the situation and there were many times when her aides didn't know what was going on.

Every day we prayed that he could just make it through the school day. When the phone rang during school hours it felt like a fog horn went off. We were always on edge just waiting for that phone to go off because Tyler was in trouble again. I hated the phone! Everything that came out of it was dreadful. Sometimes, I would stare at my phone thinking, it's about to go off again. I just know it's going to ring any second with Robin crying because she has to pick up Tyler during school again.

Our doctors' circle tour ended during this time. While network-ing with friends we discovered a doctor who came highly recom-mended. We put all our time, energy, and money (not covered by our insurance) into this doctor. We went to see him every week. He was a DAN (Defeat Autism Now) doctor of osteopathy and a board certified pediatrician and herbalist. Among his specialties were bone and cranial manipulation. Translation: Holistic Doctor. I am not really the "holistic" type of guy. But he was the only doctor who seemed to be making a difference and so I'm on board! We now did all kinds of testing, chelating, and B12 injections in his butt when he was sleeping. That was always fun. And he had a steady diet of multiple all natural supplements at every meal. The kid had more pills than both my elderly grandmothers combined.

This doctor had us jumping through hoops that were totally for-eign to me. And then there came the diet! Welcome to the gluten free, soy free, and casein free diet! Whoa boy! That was something else! Robin doesn't do anything half way especially since we were told there is absolutely no cheating on this diet. We were serious! Bought new pans, you know, because our usual pans had gluten cooked in them and there could be some micro fiber wheat germ lurking in a microscopic crevasse in the pan. By the way, casein is basically anything dairy. I didn't know that, nor what gluten was when we began. Do you know what foods contain gluten, soy, and casein? Every food ever made! With the exception of killing whatever game happened by, skinning it in a sterile area, and cooking it up in our new skillet with only salt and pepper! So gluten disappeared from our home as well as any domestic or wild life in the area.

The more the downward spiral with Tyler continued, the more we did everything we possibly could to fix him. Every day and night, Robin was immersed in a book trying to find answers. We had people from various organizations come to our home and train us for hours. Our whole family jumped into a program at Children's' Hospital where we would spend the first part of our session observing our son through a two-way mirror. Then we would go in the room with him and exercise what we had been taught. We were trained in every situation. We had homework assignments. Not just reading, but logging antecedents, reactions, solutions and outcomes to Tyler's behaviors.

Robin would often give me reading assignments. There were trips everywhere for training and testing and evaluations and you name it! Our weekly doctor visit was 40 minutes away with no traffic. Nothing was close! One time Robin took Ty to the Children's Hospital in Los Angeles. That is a two hour drive with no traffic. But when is there no traffic in LA? They did testing for four days in a row! Keep in mind that we have two other boys! One is 25 months older and the other 25 months younger than Ty. Their lives are certainly not on hold. You may be wondering if anyone works. I mean when could we? I became self-employed. Funny thing when you're self employed, if you don't work, you don't get paid. We were stretched thin and it was taxing on our family and our marriage.

Despite our best efforts, our IEP team continued to insist that Tyler was in the best placement possible. Tyler was pinned down and

33

restrained on the lawn. Then we'd say, "Really? Really!? He is in the best placement. Do you really think so? Shall we review what has happened in the past week?"

We scouted out different classes in the district and did everything we could to get him out of this horrible situation. For me, the boiling point came when I was on a business trip and the principal decided to suspend Tyler. Even though the incident was admittedly an accident, the principal spoke with her office assistant who advised her she needed to keep control and set an example. She needed to show that she would stick with her staff and show them she is supporting them.

Although it is addressed mostly to our principal, the following is a letter I sent to our IEP team and their supervisors as a result of Tyler's suspension.

Dear Team Tyler,

I have a few items for which I need some clarification. Please get back to me when you can.

Dr. Jones (not real name),

I cut my business trip short and drove home from northern California last night so I could spend the day with Tyler, who you suspended from school. I totally do not understand. What happened to all those comforting things you said to us about being on our side, and our team, and you know how we feel? You even said to me, "We would never blame Tyler for his behavior," and yet you suspend him for his behavior? How is that not blaming him for his behavior?

Apparently he's being suspended for kicking the teacher, which he didn't even know he did, and was clearly an accident. So why now? And why not suspend him for when he really acts out and kicks on purpose? Can we expect more suspensions next time he acts out? Really, I can not believe you have suspended a special-needs five-year old kindergartener who is in a class specifically designed to deal with his problems--a class where this team has placed him, and where they all have told me he belongs. And what about the timing? Begin the weekend with our kindergartener serving a suspension? And on the school day before his birthday?

So what do you want me to do with Tyler today? What do you expect me to do? I don't understand? How should I discipline him? He already thinks he's a "bad boy." He already knows he's different, has problems, and a low self-esteem. You want me to explain to him what a "suspension from school" is? A boy who hates school enough to run away from it. Do you really think that's a good idea? I can't tell you how much I disagree with this.

Team,

Please help! I really like and am grateful for each of you, even Dr. Jones, who I have a disagreement with today. We put ourselves in your hands, and our previous team, and followed every bit of counsel and recommendation. Do you really still think that Tyler is in the right place? He has no respect for his teacher and she is clearly incapable of teaching him. I see a lack of organization, creativity, basic teaching skills, and passion! She's overly concerned with what she can and cannot say what she can and cannot do. She uses the correct buzz words to make sure she's doing everything by the book. She doesn't speak to us like any member of this team. She's quite immature, and I'm not willing to wait around for some maturity process to take place while my son is in her class. What do you see? You are there assessing the teacher. Is she getting the job done to your satisfaction?

I have other questions I'll get to later, but know that, although upset, I'm really looking for answers and to understand. If I'm totally wrong, please tell me and help me understand.

Rick Daynes

My letter circulated well beyond our IEP team and inside meetings were a buzz. It led to a quickly organized and emotional IEP meeting where the District Special Education Director officiated. This was the meeting I made reference to in my Introduction where 14 people attended including our two attorneys, and I was the only man in the room. Someone once told me never to mess with a parent whose kid was threatened. Well, it was my kid who was being threatened, and I'd never before felt so much raw emotion. It was all I could do to contain myself in these meetings as the gloves had officially come off.

After the four hour IEP drama fest, the district offered us NPS (Non Public School) as they were incapable of taking care of him. They would pay to have an outside agency be responsible for teaching him. It was determined that until we found a program suitable for Tyler, he would not be in that class nor with his teacher any more. He would instead have his own classroom by himself.

What you say as a parent has some sway. But what you write has more power.

The Search for a Better School

The search for the right private school for our boy was a beast! Robin would tell you it was a nightmare. The thought of our boy meeting with one or two teachers in a closet-like room fueled the pace of our search. I wanted to completely take him out of school, but was told that was illegal unless we home schooled, which we did not want to do, but was becoming a better option every day.

Every private school we toured had something major wrong with it. Plus many of them were so far away! It felt like child abuse to put my boy on a bus for a few hours every day. Each day brought a new bad school tour, a new ugly situation, and new bad experience in and out of the education system, and life was no longer enjoyable. It hadn't been for some time.

Every minute of every day was filled with something, mostly concerning Tyler. At times it felt like there wasn't time to breathe. By the end of the day Robin and I were spent. And I mean completely exhausted. Putting the kids to bed at the end of the day was a fatiguing chore. When you are not in a good place and you are putting kids to bed who can't seem to follow the most basic rules or routines, you yell and get angry. When the kids finally got to bed, that anger and frustration would often spill into couples' time. Discussing the day's problems under these circumstances was a recipe for disaster. So our marriage suffered.

I could write volumes about this year alone. There are so many stories within stories. For example: We signed Ty up for an indoor soccer league. He's slower than all the kids, so when a kid goes whizzing past, he can't help but occasionally grab him. Robin and I had to go onto the field and remove him about half a dozen times. And then the complaints from the other parents increased. We wanted so badly for Ty to develop; we were willing to put him in situations, like soccer, that would be very uncomfortable for us. Ever heard of a kid kicked out of a soccer league twice by the age of 5? Well, that's my boy.

Parents complained openly about our boy. And then they talked to other parents who looked at our kid like he's a nut job. Then they look at you like you're a bad parent. I just want to say, "Look buddy, he's got some issues, but we're good parents and we're doing our best to teach him and solve these problems." Other times, I really just wanted to cold cock the jerk between the eyes. But then you remember that they don't understand. I've been that jerk before I'm sure. Not until you are dealing with it, will you really understand. And to understand is half the battle.

The following chapters are short, to the point, and everything I wish someone would have told me prior to our year from Hell. Enjoy!

It's ALL About the Teacher

"What do you think the teacher's gonna look like this year?"
<u>Hot for Teacher</u> *Van Halen*

Desperate times call for desperate measures. Finding placement for my boy caused Robin and me to look high and low, in every corner of the county and beyond. and leave no stone unturned. We had charts of public and private schools and how we ranked them. Every day began and ended with this giant poster board chart I constructed with all the rankings. I would kneel down in front of the chart and pray and plead for God to direct us to the right institution. You may or may not be religious, but I was becoming more religious every day. You know the saying, "there are no atheists in foxholes?" Well, this was my foxhole.

Call it an epiphany, answer to prayer, or whatever, but one day I had an experience that got me thinking that it's really all about the teacher. We were sincerely looking for a teacher, but it was jumbled with all kinds of other factors, like the campus, hours, distance, bus schedules, success rate, rankings by this organization or that, and on and on. I threw out the poster board and all the charts of all the institutions and focused on teachers. I wrote their names down, and gathered any and all information I could get about them, whether their class was full or not.

It didn't take long for us to narrow our list down. With Tyler still meeting in a closet like room with two or more teachers and specialists every day, Robin and I came together. We narrowed the search to a couple names. Our first choice was a teacher who we liked. We did not like her classroom. It was a dark and dingy trailer. Also, the kids in her class were far more handicapped than our boy. Important variables when choosing a class right? Nevertheless, we gathered good information and felt hopeful with this teacher.

The only problem was she had to be on board. I remember thinking and wholeheartedly praying that this teacher has got to want him. Even if a teacher agrees to have him in her class, how will I know if she wants him? Impossible to know, really. I can't just come out and ask her to want him. Tyler's reputation in the district was extensive, so I could not imagine any teacher wanting him.

I approached this teacher in the parking lot of her school. Probably not the best place to get the ear of a teacher, but I saw the opportunity and went for it. I wasn't sure what to say. She might have thought I was a stalker. And with all the digging we had done on her, that wasn't far off. We had met briefly several months earlier. So, I opened with that. I told her who I was and about Tyler. Emotions were surging inside of me, but I kept them in check. Although, I am sure she sensed it, I was charged up because I did not want the conversation to end without knowing if she really wanted my boy in her class. I needed to know that she wanted the challenge. That she was one of those teachers you hear about, full of passion, not willing to give up on a child.

Our conversation didn't last long, because she looked me in the eye and said, "Send him to me. I want this boy."

One school day later, our Tyler was in a new school in Ms. Esther's class. You cannot imagine the anxiety of the first day or first week. We didn't receive a call the entire week! Having previously received calls daily, this was a welcomed surprise. During the second week, curiosity was overwhelming and Robin and I went in for a visit during school. Ms. Esther explained that he was doing fine and showed us his desk and daily schedule and so forth. She never said anything about his behavior and it was driving me crazy. So I asked her. She said, "Oh that. Well, he threw a tantrum one day flopping around. I was like, this is it? This is what everyone is up in arms about? Seriously, that's all you got!? I just told him when you're ready to get back to work, I'll be over there. A few minutes later he came over to me and we got back to work."

It was at that moment I knew we had found the right teacher. I won't go into the details of the rest of his time in Ms. Esther's class, but to us it was nothing short of a series of miracles how she turned that kid around. She was a Godsend, and life at the Daynes' home improved dramatically.

It All Could Have Been Avoided

"You can't help but... with 20/20 hindsight, go back and say, 'Look, had we done something different, we probably wouldn't be facing what we are facing today."

Norman Schwarzkopf

With the 20/20 hindsight of us trying to figure out what was most important, the stunning realization?... "It all could have been avoided."

This was our assessment of what happened:

At the close of our PEPP year, just prior to moving Tyler into Kindergarten and our year from Hell, we took it upon ourselves to do a thorough search of our school district to find the ideal Kindergarten setting for our Tyler. Our IEP team wasn't giving us options, so we located all the Special Education classrooms ourselves and went to work.

What we looked at was:

The stuff on the walls and how the room was decorated

We checked how modern the classroom and school were

Proximity to our home was a big issue

And the bus! How long would Tyler's bus ride to and from school be and with how many other kids?

Do we know the psychologist, speech therapist, Principal, or anyone on the IEP team? Do we like them? Is Special Education new to this school or how long has it been there?

40

What are the kids like in this class?

Do we like the aides and how long have they been together?

We spent a considerable amount of time dissecting everything from the playground to the neighborhood to the PTA. This was our first big search for the perfect classroom. Our thought process was all about our son. We wanted to do the best thing for our boy. We left no stone unturned and we searched for the best possible fit. We met as often as we needed to, to dissect every aspect and figure out where to put our kid.

We bugged our program specialist incessantly about having options. She could see we were frustrated that we did not have a dozen different classrooms to choose from. So, to appease us, she gave us a few alternative options even though it was not her recommendation to do so, and there were no guarantees we could get into any of those optional classes.

We searched them out anyway and liked the teacher of one of these options. But the classroom... the classroom was a trailer in back of the school. The room was dark and dingy. It had a musty smell. The kids in the class were much more handicapped than our Tyler. We were offended that our program specialist set up a tour of this class. We walked out of there humbled and a little angry. Robin was crying. No way were we going to put our kid in THAT class!

We reluctantly agreed to the recommendation of our IEP team for Tyler's placement, and began the year from Hell mentioned earlier. A few months later with this program Tyler was being kept in a closet-like room by himself. We had secured attorneys and armored up to the battle for our son and his education.

But it all could have been avoided! The year from Hell and the scars it left. Tears, sleepless nights, fights, time, and money could have all been avoided! That teacher we liked, with the dark, musty classroom in back of the school, and the kids who were far worse than our child. That teacher was MS. ESTHER!

It's Still All About the Teacher

It goes without saying, doesn't it. It's all about the teacher. A no brainer right? I mean, think of the teachers you had growing up at any level. Think about those who inspired you and helped you and those who didn't. Think about the teachers who spent extra time with you or your class and legitimately cared. And think about those who did not.

For parents of kids with special needs, you will be introduced to an entire line up of specialists who will help your child. These are wonderful people who chose their field of expertise because they want to make a difference in the lives of children, who are at a disadvantage. Your son or daughter could be changed forever by the Occupational Therapist, Speech Therapist, Principal, Teacher's Aides, or School Psychologist.

As wonderful as these people are, they should not be considered when choosing placement for your kid. Do not confuse the teacher with the Physical Therapist or anyone else. Unless your choice is between two teachers who you can't decide between, then and only then should you look at other resources to sway you one way or another. The teacher is in charge of educating your child. The teacher will spend the most time with him or her and will be the biggest factor in his school year and throughout his life.

I am currently helping a friend in a situation right now. She explained to me that her son's personal aide cannot stand the Resources Specialist. The Resources Specialist, unknown to the personal aide, has voiced her displeasure of the job the personal aide is doing. Parents should not know about these little feuds, but it happens. My friend is considering moving her son to a closer school for various reasons. So I asked her, what does the Resources Specialist and aide think about the teacher? Although they are at odds, they both love the teacher.

My advice to her, was put your support behind the teacher for any problem surrounding their son and do not move him away from a great teacher in hopes of greener pastures. If you find a good teacher, take it and run! Don't give it up unless you have to. It is all about the teacher.

Myth: Our teacher and IEP team are considering all the teachers to see who will make the best match with our Anna. We are looking for the best fit. Who will little Johnny really mesh with?

I have heard that statement or variations of it so many times, it has become cliché. There are several buzz words and feel good statements in the world of education. This one sounds great to parents, but doesn't really mean much when the rubber hits the road. They do want a good fit, but they have to fill their classrooms. You cannot put 40 kids in Ms. Landers class because she rocks and 20 kids in Mr. Hans class because he sucks. Always keep in mind that principals need to fill classrooms with even amounts of kids.

In Special Education it could be worse because you are dealing with a larger geographic area, different types of classes, schools, and many other factors. Remember, they must do the math, and there will always be odd fits and bad placements. The key is to make sure it's not your kid. The 'Myth' is true a small percentage of the time. The truth is that the best teacher for Dick and Jane is most of the time the best teacher for Anna and Johnny.

If you are looking at next year's third grade teachers and they're all great, then don't worry about splitting hairs and consider yourself fortunate. If two or one or none out of three look good, you'd better get crackin'!

It's Who You Know

"What I want from each and every one of you is a hard-target search of every gas station, residence, warehouse, farmhouse, henhouse, outhouse and doghouse in that area." Deputy Marshal Samuel Gerard "The Fugitive"

Everyone has a story about the good teacher and the bad teacher. There is that great teacher who made a difference in your life and influenced or even changed you. That teacher who intervened after an altercation your son was in and decided to take care of the matter in her classroom rather than send the culprits to the office. They come in all shapes and sizes. You cannot underestimate the power of a good teacher. Getting the right teacher is everything.

So, here is your game plan for landing the best teacher. It ain't rocket science, but requires effort on your part. Don't get comfortable if your son or daughter has a great teacher this year. This demands your attention every year. Don't get lazy on this! Plenty of parents get way too complacent because their current teacher rocks and they can't imagine getting the wrong teacher the following year. Get this right and life will be sweet. Get it wrong and the opposite applies.

Ready for the non-rocket science? The secret for finding and reeling in the best teacher for your kid comes in three parts.

1. **Have a relationship with the teacher and aide(s).**

    The teachers know each other well, most of the time. Teacher relationships are not confined to school boundaries. Most teachers know multiple teachers and associate with teachers at other schools. This is especially true for the Special Education program.

    Ms. Esther had Tyler in her class for a year and a half. Ty went into 2nd grade with another dynamite teacher. How did we find her? Ms. Esther recommended her. At this point think about how close Ms. Esther is with Tyler. She has so much time and energy and love and everything invested

44

in him. She wasn't going to pass him on to anyone but the best. When you get a recommendation like that, it is as good as gold.

Plus everyone on our IEP team agreed. We double-checked with parents who had their kids in her room previously. Stars all around! And a huge plus is that although he went into a main-stream class with an aide, we kept him at that same school. If anything went wrong, Ms. Esther's class was two doors away and she was "Johnny on the Spot."

2. **Have a relationship with the Principal and as many administrators as possible.**

3. **Join the 'Pick-A-Littles.'**

Every school on earth has at least one and often several groups of women who are seriously dialed in. Teachers love them because they volunteer hours in their classrooms. Administrators love them because they run the PTA, throw parties, events, and fundraisers. You love them for several reasons, number one being because they are the ultimate source of ALL INFORMATION.

When I was a kid, my parents stuck my brother and me in the musical, "The Music Man." If you are not familiar with it, it is the story of a slick salesman who enters the town of River City, Iowa to sell his "boys band" program, which is really a scam. In any case, as a kid, the most amusing part for me was the group of women lead by the Mayor's wife, Eulalie MacKecknie Shinn. This group of women had their noses in everyone's business in the town. They knew all, gossiped incessantly, and sang this infectious song that mimicked a brood of hens clucking, picking, and shaking their tail feathers. My favorite version of the song is the one starring Gonzo from the Muppets if you can find it some-place.

My brother and I began to notice the real life situation of the Pick-A-Littles. Every time we waited for my mother who was having a conversation with a friend, we would

45

sing, *"Pick a little, talk a little, pick a little, talk a little, cheep cheep cheep, talk a lot, pick a little more."* You've got to sing it in your best falsetto. When one woman went to the bathroom, but had to be accompanied by her friends, we sing, *"Pick a little, talk a little, pick a little, talk a little, cheep cheep cheep, talk a lot, pick a little more."* The idea caught on with more friends and basically any time there was a group of women, you could sing the *Pick-a-Little chorus.*

I should mention that the school Pick-a-Littles have, over the years, gone by several other pet names depending on the group. There was the Pink Ladies, Call Me Girls, PTA groupies, Carnies, Fashion Four, Socialites, etc. You get the picture, all are Pick-A-Littles. And although we poke fun at the Pick-A-Littles, we love them! We love them for several reasons. They know the strengths and weaknesses of every teacher and administrator, the exact bell times, rules to all recess games, and every kid who has a peanut allergy. They are easily approachable and love to share any and all information.

And they love you! You are the dad with the special needs kid or the kid who is having a hard time and needs help in a certain area. You are 'that' dad taking a special interest in his kid. You are reaching out, looking for answers. And the Pick-A-Littles eat that up! They are full of compassion and love and they make things happen!

You may be saying to yourself, "great, they can tell me who the best teacher is and what will be new at this year's Fall Festival. But they cannot get that teacher for my child."

Myth: In our school you are not allowed to request a teacher for the next year.

WRONG! How do you think the placement process happens? They throw the names in a hat or the computer randomly organizes the classrooms for the next year? No. It is determined by the teachers and administrators. Your kid's teacher has spent a year teaching your kid. He or she is invested and loves your kid. But the teacher has several kids they feel that way about and they all can't go to the same best teacher.

46

Look at the main stream Pick-A-Littles. I've known hundreds over the years and they frequently get the teacher they want for their kid every year. No principal or teacher will ever admit they played favorites, but don't kid yourself. Pick-A-Littles provide invaluable service to the classroom and school and have built solid relationships in the process. Granting a favor to the dedicated Pick-A-Little at the end of the year is a given. You don't have time to be a Pick-A-Little, and you're the wrong sex. But, do you have a relationship with the teacher and or principal? If so, you're golden.

Oh-Oh-Oh O'Reilly, O'Reilly!
(sing in O'Reilly Auto Parts jingle voice)

Going into second grade my oldest boy (not special needs) was assigned to a first and second grade combination class. This didn't sit well with us as our boy is very smart and could easily keep up with the third graders and beyond. So the idea of him in the same classroom with first graders was unsettling. We had heard good things about the teacher, Mrs. O'Reilly, and decided to chill and see how it went.

Our first parent teacher conference came and both Robin and I attended. Mrs. O'Reilly took us through his scores and projects and behaviors and he was excelling at everything. I was beaming because my kid was smart and this would be a short conference. I mean, what do we really have to discuss? I was about to exit my seat when she announced she had concerns and a plan. I thought maybe she was going to make a joke or something. The kid is on top of his game. What more could anyone want?

She told us she was worried he might get bored in class or disengaged. Then she said something that I'll never forget. "It doesn't matter if he's the smartest kid in school, it's my job to challenge him." She asked us for suggestions to keep him engaged and challenged. She wanted real growth and to push our son to be as good as he could be. She made and executed a plan for this kid to reach his potential. Turns out Mrs. O'Reilly was freaken' awesome!

A couple years later at the end of the year, Mrs. O'Reilly received her second teacher of the year award. That same week and possibly the same day she received that award, she was given her walking papers. You see, during the budget cuts of a few years ago, every teacher who didn't have tenure was given a pink slip. This happened two years in a row. All these great teachers went into the summer break not knowing if they were going to have jobs when school began in the fall. It's like a game. Pass out the pink slips and then figure out finances and see if we can bring back the younger teachers. Yes, that's right, fire the best teacher in the school because she hasn't been around long enough. But that is what we have come to expect from our education system.

Fast forward a couple years and our Tyler has made huge strides. He is out of his Autism Spectrum Disorder class and is mainstreaming with an aide in second grade! This is nothing short of a miracle. His teacher is Mrs. Krumenacker and she is dynamite! You will recall that Ms. Esther recommended her and we were fortunate enough for Tyler to have her for second and third grade! Midway through third grade, we were on the hunt for his fourth grade teacher. So naturally, we met with Mrs. Krumenacker to get her thoughts on possible options.

I told her that we would really love Tyler to stop bussing so far away everyday and attend his home school in our neighborhood. There is a teacher there, who we think would be great for Tyler. She asked for the name, and I said, Mrs. O'Reilly. Mrs. Krumenacker then said, "I think Lauren would be a wonderful teacher for Tyler. " I reply, "Oh, you know her?" then she said, "Yes, Lauren was in my wedding."

In the county in which we live, there are 42 school districts. Within our district there are 26 elementary schools. I do not know how many teachers there are, but it's no small number. And within all those teachers, the two best that I know are at different schools. Now, not only do they know each other, they are BFF's. Coincidence? I think not! See #1 above, where we list sources for finding a good teacher. Birds of a feather flock together. Good teachers, being good friends is no surprise.

Getting your Special Ed kid to switch schools and land him with the teacher you want is no easy task. Next thing to do was ask Mrs. O'Reilly what she thought. She had met Ty a couple times very briefly. I gave her Tyler's story in a nutshell and asked her what she thought about being our prime target to be his next teacher. She was predictably excited to take on the challenge. She also responded by telling me about when she was in school having a difficult decision between teaching Special Education or General Education. Any mainstream teacher who wants a special education kid in her class is something special. Most of the time that means extra time, extra problems, and all the issues that come with one kid, in addition to what you already have. Most Special Education teachers have a heart of gold, so it was no surprise to hear Mrs. O'Reilly seriously considered going in that direction.

When all was said and done, we opted not to transfer Tyler to our neighborhood school. The reason is because we did not accomplish #2 (see #2 above). We did not have a good relationship with our local principal. The year prior, we decided to hold our third son back and have him repeat Kindergarten. He was a November birthday and the youngest in his grade plus he has Aspergers, so it was an easy decision. However, the principal did not agree and we felt a bit unstable with her.

If we transferred to our neighborhood school, we were at the mercy of our principal as to whose class Tyler ended up in. With four different fourth grade teachers, it was too much of a gamble that he would end up with Mrs. O'Reilly. We did keep rule #2 in effect at his current school. It was easy, as he was a really cool principal. We knew exactly where and who he would be with. Too bad we failed on #2 at our home school. It could have been huge. Perhaps Rodney Dangerfield said it best, "Look out for number one and try not to step in number two."

The Aides

Teachers' aides are the unsung heroes in the world of Special Education. In many cases they are as important as, or even more important than the teacher. It all depends on what type of program and situation your child is in. The aides should be a reflection of the teacher. The teacher is the quarterback. She calls the plays and generals the aides (offensive line). It does not matter if you have a Joe Montana in there, if you don't control the line of scrimmage, you are going to lose. And the aides do exactly that. They control the line.

They make the classroom flow. They spend the one-on-one time with your kid. They work with, and protect, the quarterback. Want to find a good teacher? If she has a team of aides, find out how long they have been together. A good teacher is going to do everything she can to land and retain good aides. If the aides have been with the teacher a long time, that means good communication, good relationships, good team.

If the aides circulate in and out a lot, you need to find out why. There are many valid explanations for this, such as your district automatically rotates aides. A lot of the aides are young, so they leave for school, get married, change careers, etc. If you cannot find out why aides move in and out of a certain teacher's class, that means no one is talking. What that means is aides are asking to be transferred out. That means the aides don't like how she runs the class and bad relationships are the result. A teacher who doesn't have good relationships with her aides is not going to have good relationships with parents. Take a pass on that class.

I realize I refer to teachers and aides as "she." I do this simply because it's convenient and most teachers are female. I don't have any problem with men in any capacity in education and don't favor one over the other unless being a certain sex gives you an edge with a certain kid, which happens all the time. And while I'm on the subject, the first aide we ever had was a young man, maybe 20ish, in school, trying to figure out what to be in life. He was a brand new aide who was trained while working with my boy, and he was awesome! Boris! Are you out there? You were killer awesome (canyon echo yelling)!

The only sub-par experience I've had with an aide or aides, was when I had a problem with the teacher. Coincidence? Again, I think not! Remember, the teacher's aide is a reflection of the teacher. Those experiences are rare for us because we follow the steps to grab the best teacher, right?

Just think of the teacher's aide as a Pick-A-Little with half the training of a teacher. Many are in school to be teachers and some are even retired teachers who want to get back into the classroom and make a difference but do not want the responsibilities of a teacher. In short, you love them. You need to know them and they know you. Currently, my Tyler has an aide and mainstreams in a regular elementary class. She is with him more than anyone other than his mother. If you are in our situation, you know how important that aide is. You better put her next to the teacher in your number one on the priority relationship list.

IGNORANCE WARNING: I do not know everything on the aide warning.

AIDE WARNING: I am pretty sure this is nationwide, but teachers' aides are not allowed to attend IEP meetings, or any meetings for that matter. Pretty lame considering many aides know the child better than the teacher. Not only are they not to attend meetings, but contact between parents and aides is discouraged to forbidden. Aides work with the teacher and the teacher has the relationship with the parents. Given the importance and amount of time our aide spends with our kid, you can probably guess what my take is on this subject.

My wife and I know Tyler's aide well. We know her kids, hobbies, and interests. We have each other's cell numbers and emails and openly communicate. She is the first person I check with when anything good or bad happens. She texts us pictures and updates all the time and we love it. She is on the front line with our son every day. We would be foolish not to have a good relationship with her. Tyler's teacher probably knows that we communicate with her often and probably doesn't care or may encourage it.

But that is not the norm! Most teachers are not like that. In fact, that kind of contact is taboo. I'm not going to ask Tyler's teacher if we can communicate with her aide. If she just says that's fine, we're already communicating. If she follows the proper rules and procedures and says no, we're going to do it anyway. Most likely she is fine with it, but asking her that question puts her in a bad place because she's supposed to say we should communicate with her regarding Tyler. If she does not say that, then she could get in trouble. So this is one of those situations where you keep a low profile and don't say or ask anything of anyone.

As far as your IEP team goes, never ever under any circumstances let any one of them know you communicate with your child's aide other than brief conversations. Not unless you want her to get fired. And believe me, it happens. Ty's aide knows anything she says to us will never be repeated and the same goes for her. Trust is a must! We had an email thread going around our IEP team recently concerning Tyler. I would forward them to our aide and she and Robin and I communicated about them. But the team would never know. And we'll keep it that way.

Correspondence

You followed the steps and hopefully got the best teacher for your kid. There are no guarantees of course, as every kid and teacher is different. But you put in the effort needed and you feel good about the coming school year. Hopefully, what that means is little to no drama, red tape, incidences, issues, relocating, etc. You don't have time for that. But here's what you have time for:

1. Meet the teacher. Typically, teachers come in to set up their classrooms a day to a week before the school year begins. See if you can set up a brief meeting with her during that time. If not then, sometime as early as possible in the school year. Take your wife with you! Dress nice and do everything you can to make a good first impression. Talk about her and get to know her. Don't get into the issues your child has. The teacher will be expecting that, but let the conversation about your kid be <u>minimal and positive</u>.

You are about to begin a new year. Everything should be positive. Let the teacher and your kid begin without preconceived notions, within reason. A lot of kids especially in Special Ed have issues you need to get out in front of, or nip in the bud. Your wife, more than you will have the urge to talk about past struggles, disabilities, and issues. Keep it to a minimum and keep it positive! The teacher is smart. Though she hasn't seen your kid yet, she has experience and this isn't her first rodeo. If she wants to know about her new student, she has already done so. Remember, teachers talk. Plus, she has access to the IEP transcripts and knows the IEP goals. Hopefully, she hasn't dug in too deep and the student and the teacher will begin the year with a blank slate.

Your objectives for this first meeting are as follows:

A. Get to know the teacher on a personal level. You want her to be comfortable with you and visa versa.

B. Let her know that you and your wife are an inseparably strong TEAM! You don't need to tell her that. She will see it in the way you treat your wife and that you are there for your child.

C. Open the lines of communication. Personal emails and cell numbers are exchanged. But remember this! You do not have time to deal with the day-to-day events in school. So this is the time to say something like: Ms. Othmar, I am pretty busy and Robin (wife) is fantastic with Tyler. I do want to be involved though. If there is any email correspondence, could you CC me? And of course my line is always open if you need to discuss anything.

She won't call you as all phone conversations will go to your wife. But she knows that you are open, on top of things, and serious. This will free you up to work and do your thing, but still send the message to everyone that you are connected and care. Occasionally respond or send an email to Ms. Othmar. Always CC your wife and when appropriate your IEP team. <u>And always be thankful and ap-</u>

preciative in every email or communication. Even if problems arise and you have differences, find something complimentary to say.

"The smallest act of kindness is worth more than the grandest intention." ~ *Oscar Wilde*

You should also give two to three gifts to the teacher every year. Generally speaking, this is your wife's department. Women are much better and more inclined to give gifts. I am including it here because we need to <u>support it</u>. One for Christmas or Hanukah is mandatory. One for the end of the year and even for her birthday is always nice. It doesn't have to be big or expensive. It's the thought that counts.

The same rules apply for the aide(s). You do not need to go overboard. If there are six aides in the class, they will understand if they don't all get something. If you could find a group gift, you're golden. If your wife has time and wants to volunteer in the classroom or school regularly or on occasion, get behind that. The benefits of selfless service are immeasurable. Don't worry if she joins the Pick-A-Littles. That's a good thing.

Warning

For your wife and maybe for you, the amount of time spent searching for something is directly proportional to how important it is. Finding the proper placement for your handicapped daughter is massive! It really cannot be measured. If you do not have a clear choice of placement in your district, and your IEP team tells you there are a few options, your wife will undergo the search to end all searches.

Let me save you some serious time, energy, and arguments with your wife. You need to convince your sweetheart in the most sincere and loving way you can possibly muster, that finding placement for your special child is absolutely all about the teacher. OK, maybe it's not all about the teacher. But, actually it is! It is all about the teacher. Nothing else matters! The school psychologist, program director, classroom colors, OT, PT, peers, income of surrounding neighborhood, old boyfriend has a kid at that school and it's on a fault line, etc. doesn't amount to anything, when compared to the teacher.

Your child's placement is paramount! If you cannot mutually understand that it's all about the teacher, then you could make the wrong choice and your wife will have you on *"a hard-target search of every gas station, residence, warehouse, farmhouse, henhouse, outhouse and doghouse in that area." Deputy Marshal Samuel Gerard, The Fugitive*

The Run-Down

1. Be skeptical about where your IEP wants to place your child. The wrong placement can mean disaster.

2. Don't worry about the school, resources, personnel, specialist, etc. **It's All About The Teacher.**

3. Most teachers are good, especially special education teachers.

4. Top resources to find and reel in the best teacher:

   A. Have a relationship with the teacher and aide(s).

   B. Have a relationship with the principal and as many administrators as possible.

   C. Join the Pick-A-Littles.

5. Despite what anyone says, you can get the teacher you want a lot of the time.

6. The best teacher for Sally and Erick is most likely the best teacher for your kid.

7. Teachers' aides are huge. Communicate with them.

8. Meet the new teacher before school begins. Your objectives:

   A. Get to know the teacher on a personal level.

B. Let her know that you and your wife are an inseparably strong TEAM!

C. Open the lines of communication.

9. Save yourself the headache. It is all about the teacher.

Reality Check

"It's the end of the world as we know it, and I feel fine." R.E.M.

Our Tyler was diagnosed with Autism at age 4. Our Jeremiah was diagnosed with Aspergers at age 6. Our Eli was diagnosed with Down Syndrome when my wife was 20 weeks pregnant. Differing disabilities under different circumstances, yet they surprisingly share common threads. Whatever your circumstances, be cognizant of the phases of your new reality.

Phase One

Denial

It Ain't Just a River in Egypt

Our first son was as precocious as they come. Walking, talking, reading, he excelled beyond most kids his age. He didn't even talk like a kid and could communicate with any adult on many subjects. When he was three I took him to a San Diego Padres baseball game. The Padre employees selected him to be the play-ball kid. Before the game the kid walks out to home plate with a microphone and yells "play ball!" The rule is the kid has to be at least five years old. Because Jefferson was tall and spoke like an adult, he pulled it off, like a pro I might add, at three. The next year, as a four year old he went to the public announcer booth to introduce the leadoff batter for the 5th inning. "Leading off for the Padres, first baseman, Adrian Gonzales!" Again, the age eligible to do that was seven.

We had to start him in school a year early and could have started him two years early. He is maybe the youngest in his grade, but you couldn't tell. Academically, physically, athletically, and socially, he's right up there. We have several "Jeffersonisms" written down, which is when he would say something totally unnatural for his age. For example, when he was three, he explained to his grandparents how George Lucas created Star Wars in 1976, or whenever that was. I'll have to ask him. Around that same time period I remember Jefferson at the dinner table pleading for a salad like a normal kid would ask for ice cream. Yes, he even ate like an adult. A health concientious adult I should say.

So when Tyler came along just 25 months later we dubbed him our "normal kid." We expected him to develop slower than Jefferson of course, but when he was two and three years old several red flags went up. I could see it, but because our number one was so advanced, I had little to compare number two to. At age four we put him in preschool. The differences between Tyler and every other kid was plain to see.

My wife saw it clearly, but I was in denial. Having a precocious first born didn't help. But I really didn't think anything was wrong. My second son reminded me of me. Whenever my wife would complain or give me examples of Tyler's abnormal behavior, I'd say, or at least think, "I did the same thing when I was his age. So he's a little aggressive, a bit aloof, doesn't like to do this or that, and has these quirky behaviors, I did the same thing."

Justification

Justification is denial's greatest tool. The more you use it, the sharper it becomes and the easier it is to use. I used it so often that it no longer sat in my tool bag, but my back pocket. My boy could do no wrong as I could explain away every abnormal behavior he had. It's not something you think about. It is a totally natural response.

Even after a self realization of the way I justified everything with Tyler, I did it again when our school wanted to evaluate Ty's little brother. "Come on Robin, there is nothing wrong with this kid. The only reason they even wanted to evaluate him was because his older brother has issues. So he (Jeremiah) flaps his hands and has some quirky behaviors. You're telling me normal kids don't do that? He's smart! Look, these ladies who evaluate these kids...it's their job to find something wrong with them."

How about our Eli? He can't have Down Syndrome, we already have two boys in Special Education! We are healthy athletic people! We have great genes! There is nothing in our bloodlines to suggest this is even possible. Robin's mom at age 46 was 11 years older than Robin when she had a baby! They gave her a one in three chance of having a baby with Down Syndrome! And did she? Nope.

Even when we took every test and the chances were 100% that Eli would have Down Syndrome... And by the way, that's the reason we took every test. Because, I could still reason it away with test results that were 99% accurate. Ahhh, how I love justification. I sound brilliant and funny when I do it too.

But I digress. Let's get back to Tyler. This was my boy! I could relate to this kid. He looked more like me, acted more like me. He was a chip off the old block! I was sure he would grow up as healthy and happy as his dad.

Robin on the other hand did not see things my way, so I dug in to defend my position. She researched and read books about Autism and Aspergers. She would show me the symptoms of all these disorders and relate them to Tyler. She'd say, "That's Tyler, that's exactly what he does." Then I'd say, "So he's a little off. He's fine, I was the same way." The more I said and thought that, the more I believed it. I was digging in. The more I dug in, the bigger my hole became. I mean come on. Have you seen the list of symptoms for "Oppositional Defiant Disorder?" It pretty much covers every kid alive at some point.

I did not want a special needs kid. I became more obstinate in thinking something might be wrong with him. Sure he's different, but he'll snap out of it. He'll be fine. And my hole continued to get deeper which increased my distance from reality and my wife. She knew Tyler needed help. And I became so good at justifying that denial became my reality.

Phase Two
Acceptance

"If you can't accept losing, you can't win" Vince Lombardi

According to the National Institute of Mental Health, "Mental disorders are common among children in the United States, and can be particularly difficult for the children themselves and their caregivers. While mental disorders are widespread, the main burden of illness is concentrated among those suffering from a seriously debilitating mental illness. Just over 20 percent (or 1 in 5) children, either currently or at some point during their life, have had a seriously debilitating mental disorder."[2] Sooner or later you will figure out that your child is that one in five. Perhaps you conceded that notion to your wife or a relative. Maybe a friend has steered you in the right direction. It's always fun when an outside observer says to you, "you know there is something wrong with your kid, right?" Eventually your child's behaviors overpower your justifications and denial. You become increasingly aware with every act of acknowledgement. Awareness leads to acceptance. Hopefully, it didn't take too long because the faster you get to phase two, the better.

Tyler was finally evaluated by doctors, psychologists, and the school district, after I got a clue. You name it we did it in order to figure this kid out. Once we started that process, we were on the road to recovery. Now, don't get me wrong here. The road to recovery is long with plenty of speed bumps, hills, mountains, and spacious valleys. But acceptance puts you and your kid at the gateway.

For me, acceptance should have come much earlier. You are not going to help your child get better until you accept that she has a disability. The earlier you come to terms with that, the faster you can begin to help him. The earlier the diagnoses, means the earlier the treatment. If you are on the fence with your kid, get him evaluated regardless of which way you are leaning. If we are talking about a child, don't play the let's wait and see if he snaps out of it game. The early developmental stages are critical for growth.

Phase Three
Fear

"Holy handicap Batman! What am I going to do now! I have a special needs child!"

This kind of thing only happens to other people. It doesn't happen to me! What the heck happens now! How will this impact my life? What will everyone think? Will I be taking care of this kid forever? How did I find myself in this situation? Will he be a thug and end up in prison? Will he be violent? What kind of demand will this have on my wife? How does special education work? Will that small bus be pulling up to my house? Do I live within a good school district? Should we home-school him? Will we be able to take him in public?

Will he be able to do anything unsupervised? Will someone have to watch her 24/7? Will kids make fun of him? How can I protect her? Will I have the patience for him? What kind of money is this going to cost me? Any free services? What about private school or care takers? Can we travel with him? Will she embarrass us? Why is this happening to us? What caused this? Is there something wrong with me or my wife or the combination of the both of us that we cannot create a normal child? Is this going to totally suck? Will this totally suck for the rest of my life? What about potty training? And the list goes on and on and on....

The fear phase actually begins the first time you consider something might be wrong. It is a contributing factor in the denial phase. I list it at phase three because fear escalates after complete acceptance. That's when it really hits the fan. When the reality of your situation has sunk in and you are thrust into something you never considered. This is that moment when the gauntlet of questions runs through your head. Sleepless nights are common. Soul searching takes the place of other activities. And you find yourself alone more. Or at least you feel alone.

When we found out Eli had Down Syndrome, it was really tough. There were some dark times. Robin was already having the worst pregnancy ever. Prior to her pregnancy, she was working out at 5:30AM every morning. She was working part time, had projects all over the place, had energy galore, and loving life! I watched this pregnancy reduce this strong woman to the point where pulling herself out of bed at 9:00AM, 10:00AM, or any hour, took every ounce of energy and emotion she had. You can only imagine how adding a Down Syndrome diagnosis can make that situation even more grim.

Do you know what it's really all about? This fear factor causes friction in solid relationships, stress, ulcers, and grown men to run! Do you realize what it's about? It's only one little thing. One small thing that people let control them and cause anxiety to no end. It's ridiculous! Are you sitting down? Are you ready for this? Because this causes people to cry and plead and agonize. It is this one little emotion. Fear of the UNKNOWN!

That's all! Fear of the unknown. OOOOOH, so scared of what we don't know, it drives us nuts! All those questions above race through our minds and we don't have solid answers. For the most part, getting solid answers takes time because, no matter the disability, every child is different and you never know the outcome. Same goes for any kid for that matter. You never really know what you're going to get.

We spent months battling Robin's pregnancy with its depression and emotional pitfalls. I can't tell you how many days I'd wake up and be in a daze thinking how can this be happening? I have two kids in special education and now I'm going to have a child with Down Syndrome! I have had little to no experience with Down Syndrome. Initially all I could think about was a fat kid sticking his tongue out slobbering gibberish.

Then my thoughts went to how much this kid was going to function and will I be changing his diapers when he's a teenager. Then I graduated to, I can forget about ever living alone with my wife. He'll be with us forever. Isn't that just in our nature? Take a bit of bad news and let your mind run in the wrong direction. Natural human tendencies suck sometimes. Most of this is brought on by the simple fear of the unknown. Sure people tell you things will be fine and give you encouragement, but you figure it's just that, compassionate encouragement.

Even when Robin was in the delivery room about to deliver Eli six weeks premature, the nurses paint this doom and gloom picture. They have to. They must prepare you by telling you everything that can possibly go wrong. For a six-week premature infant with Down Syndrome, it's a lengthy list.

As bad as I was, Robin was worse. Generally speaking, women out worry men. Robin was in a fragile state. Good news for me is that I spent so much time helping her to be positive, it rubbed off on me. Speaking of natural tendencies, this is one of our good ones. When your wife is down, you are up! Because you have to be! All of a sudden we are full of cheer and encouragement and love. Everything is going to be great. We are going to love this child, and it will be the best thing that has ever happened to us. If you say it enough you start to believe it. You wait to be alone before the pessimistic thoughts get your head.

After weeks in the NICU, we finally took Eli home. With mom and baby at home the healing and bonding process accelerated and Eli's personality begin to come out. Fast forward two years and I can tell you without any reservation that we hit the jackpot! This kid is fantastic in every way! It's hard to explain, and I'll get into this later, but he is so stinkin awesome! Robin and I often laugh about what basket cases we were. She would say, "What were we so worried about? Really, what were we so worried about!" Just because you haven't been there doesn't mean it's a bad place.

Perhaps John Lennon said it best. "It's fear of the unknown. The unknown is what it is. And to be frightened of it is what sends everybody scurrying around chasing dreams, illusions, wars, peace, love, hate, all that--it's all illusion. Unknown is what it is. Accept that it's unknown and it's plain sailing. Everything is unknown--then you're ahead of the game. That's what it is. Right?"

Phase Four
Life

"No thanks, I choose life" Sid the Sloth, Ice Age

This book is about living a meaningful and smarter life as a parent with special needs children. Whoever said knowing is half the battle wasn't the parent of a disabled kid. For us, once we know we have a disabled kid, the battle begins. I began this book by telling you these are lessons I wish someone had sat me down and told me at the beginning of our journey. And understanding this is important. As always, depending on your situation you will experience the following in varying degrees.

Your Wife Will Change

When I was thinking about getting married some time ago, I attended a lecture by a marriage/relationship expert. When the guy finished speaking, he opened it up to questions. There were a lot of dating couples and engaged couples in the audience and they seemed to be eager to ask questions. So I sat back and took note.

One guy stood up and asked, "Should we wait awhile to have kids so my wife and I can get to know each other better first?" All the other questions had some kind of pause, or the speaker would repeat it so everyone in the audience would hear the question. But not with this question. The response was immediate. "Why would you do that? Your wife is going to change several times over during the course of your marriage and you will have the opportunity to get to know her every time she changes."

It's no secret that women tend to change while men stay the same. You don't have to search hard to find a joke about how women marry hoping he will change, but he doesn't. And men marry hoping she will never change, but she does. Those jokes are funny because there is truth to it. But not until I heard that speaker talk seriously about it, did I consider how my wife might change and what effect it would have on our relationship.

You have probably seen your wife change and expect her to change again. You are ready for it. But the transformation that will occur, when she has a special needs child, will put all other changes in the negligible category. See section "Mama Bear."

You Will Change

Good Timber

by Douglas Malloch

The tree that never had to fight
For sun and sky and air and light,
But stood out in the open plain
And always got its share of rain,
Never became a forest king
But lived and died a scrubby thing.

The man who never had to toil
To gain and farm his patch of soil,
Who never had to win his share
Of sun and sky and light and air,
Never became a manly man
But lived and died as he began.

Good timber does not grow with ease:
The stronger wind, the stronger trees;
The further sky, the greater length;
The more the storm, the more the strength.
By sun and cold, by rain and snow,
In trees and men good timbers grow.

Where thickest lies the forest growth,
We find the patriarchs of both.
And they hold counsel with the stars
Whose broken branches show the scars
Of many winds and much of strife.
This is the common law of life.

Your life is about to become or has already become more of a rollercoaster. You will go through the refiners fire of steep drops into deep valleys at break neck speeds, and an instant later fly to peaks you didn't think possible. Your lows will be lower and your highs higher. You will change with these experiences into the patriarch mentioned in the poem. Enjoy the coaster and embrace the change.

The Run Down

1. Life has thrown you a curve ball.

2. Phase One: Denial. It's easy to become an expert.

    A. Justification is denial's greatest tool.

3. Phase Two: Acceptance. The sooner you face reality, the better.

4. Phase Three: Fear. It is ALL about the UNKNOWN.

5. Phase Four: Life. Understand.

    A. Life as you know it, is no longer.

    B. Your wife will change, enjoy it.

    C. You will change, embrace it.

Karate Kid

"Lesson not just karate only. Lesson for whole life. Whole life have a balance. Every-thing be better. Understand?" Mr. Miyagi, The Karate Kid

During the 2008 Summer Olympics in Beijing China, Michael Phelps stunned the world by collecting eight gold medals. A feat never before realized. We learned a lot about this athlete as there was no shortage of interviews with him, his mom, and others who surrounded him.

His mother told us of the struggles she had with Michael growing up. He was a very different kid and her trials with him resonated with us. She eventually found that the pool offered a reprieve, a sanctuary for Michael, where he could get out his frustrations, and feel comfortable. He talked about his lane and how he felt more comfortable there. To say that he excelled in the pool would be an understatement of course.

This story gave us hope. Michael Phelps had his pool, but could we find something for our Tyler? We weren't looking to create an Olympic athlete. We just wanted to find something where he could get out his energy, emotions, and find solace and peace in that little body. Heck, I'd settle for anything he halfway liked to do.

In our efforts to give Tyler anything and everything that could help him, we found a local karate program. I'm not sure how it's funded, but it's free to the handicap people in it. I'm not sure how a lot of programs are funded that we looked into, that were free for us, but God bless those who create, fund, run, and volunteer to help these special kids. Whoever you are out there, I hope your life is blessed immensely for the money and service you give.

This again was one of those programs where we just didn't know if it was worth it. Ty spent most of his time running away from instructors, hiding behind equipment, making faces in the mirror, running into the bathroom, and doing everything but what he should be doing. We of course were constantly running around after him, encouraging, coaxing, and bribing him to participate.

As if the weekdays were not enough, we were now exhausting ourselves on Saturdays, putting him in Karate. This class had every handicap represented from Autism to Down Syndrome and our kid was easily the most disruptive. It was embarrassing even among parents of the handicapped. Instructors and volunteers would tag team and team up on our boy to get him to participate.

He was taking up their time and energy when it could be used on other kids. Tyler did not even want to go to Karate. We made him. Why did we subject him, ourselves, and the instructors to this? Why did we go through this? He was getting nothing from it. In fact, his behavior in class just got worse. We went every week in hopes that he would turn it around? We wondered if it would ever click inside his brain and provide some kind of change.

The Tournament

Every few months they would announce a tournament. They did have a place in tournaments for special needs kids, but we felt Tyler was in no way ready for a tournament. One Saturday morning, Robin announced to the family that we were all going to Tyler's karate tournament. I nearly choked on my toast. Were we really going to subject ourselves to this? He probably wouldn't participate? I was motivated by Robin's go for it attitude, so why not, what's the worst that could happen?

The tournament was held in a large gymnasium. All the mats were spread out on a basketball floor with stands on both sides. On the other side of the bleachers existed another basketball court that participants could use to warm up, meet, go through their pre-match rituals. What this meant to our family was chaos. In order to contain Ty, we needed a small place with few hiding places. This was just the opposite with vast spaces and plenty of nooks and crannies. There were lots of "off limits" areas which Ty seemed to find frequently. For a good hour we spent chasing, corralling, apologizing to parents and people for whatever Ty was getting into.

When the time had come for Ty to perform, he was running around outside and then in the bathroom and then under some mats and disrupting some other karate students to the point I boiled over. I grabbed him, got down on his level and told him to get out there with his class or all privileges for the day would be lost. Sometimes that approach worked and sometimes it didn't. In this case it did!

So off Tyler went to his class. He sat as patiently as I can remember for almost a minute before darting somewhere, but I anticipated the move and was there to redirect him back to the mat. His instructor called for him first, no doubt because he knew Ty was not going to hang around long. The performance commenced and Tyler was on stage. He successfully blocked several shots from his instructor, Mr. Kats. He then proceeded to deliver several punches and kicks to the pads. Several unsolicited blows came spontaneously, but we didn't care. We were excited to see him out there doing most of what he was supposed to do.

When he finished, he retired to the mat in his proper place for maybe 10 seconds. Then he was off again. I found him and told him how happy I was and how well he did, trying to get some kind of reaction out of him. He was more interested in other things going on. I kept him occupied long enough for the awards for the special needs kids, which happened right after they performed. Good thing too.

After several attempts to get Ty on the mat for the awards, he reluctantly went. When two boys his age were presented with trophies, he again bolted, but this time out of frustration. He was upset because he wanted a trophy badly! Tyler did not understand that the 1st place trophy was always given last. And now he was running in the opposite direction. Again, I anticipated his move and intercepted him to the whining and frustration he so frequently exemplified.

I turned him around and pointed his head across the gymnasium. His instructor was holding the first place trophy. He yelled to Tyler, "Do you want your trophy?" And then it happened. That one moment you'll remember for the rest of your life. Time stood still. All the frustration, anguish, and effort were worth the price. Tyler stood in his Karate uniform with his white belt in total disarray at center stage. He was barely able to hold the gleaming gold and green trophy that was almost as tall as he was. He bear hugged the skyscraping trophy as it was the only way he could keep it off the ground. And he beamed while the crowd gave him a rousing ovation.

Nothing could disrupt this special moment. That image of him will forever be engrained in my mind. But then Ty's younger brother was holding himself and screaming that he was about to pee his pants! So we ran to the little boys room. Upon exiting the bathroom we searched for Tyler. When we found him, I discovered an even sweeter scene than the trophy presentation. With tears flowing like a fountain, Robin was on her knees hugging her special boy. At that moment I realized as much as I had put into Tyler, it did not compare with what his mother had sacrificed for him. And the elation I felt when he reacted to receiving that trophy, couldn't be measured on any earthly scale for what his mother felt.

They both walked toward me, my boy still beaming, my wife still sobbing. I embraced them both and we shared a moment that will forever be with us. Robin said, I want to get his name engraved on the trophy. There was a little booth where someone engraved trophies. I think the cost was $10 bucks. At that moment, I would have paid $1,000.

Screen Sitters

"Most people gaze neither into the past nor the future; they explore neither truth nor lies. They gaze at the television." Radiohead

I'm sounding the alarm on this! Actually, the alarm has been sounded. But I am joining the fight! You may be thinking epidemic is a strong word for what I am about to say, but I'm totally serious. Also, I'm a little guilty as well because it's so easy to fall into. It's called SCREEN SITTERS, and it has already swept your home, my home, and the majority of the modern world.

I have poured way too many hours into online research studying why people pour way too many hours into, well, online. Not because I need to be educated, although I do. Simply because I am totally blown away at the information I have come across. There is too much information for this book's purposes. But let me give you the highlights and a little homework.

Homework: Google "how much screen time does the average kid spend a day." Spend next 20 minutes reading and scraping your jaw off the floor. I have my favorite studies and articles, but there is always new information and it is constantly changing. Plus this information is easy to find. The highlights below come from the website: makinghealtheasier.org/getmoving[3]

I like this website, not because of the statistics, they are easy to find and do not vary much. I like it because it offers alternatives and helps to 'the screen sitter epidemic.' Highlights: Depending on age (6-18) and which study(s) you looked at, kids spend 6-8 hours on AVERAGE in front of a screen every day. Many websites and studies suggested even longer amounts of time, especially for early teens. But I am really having a hard time wrapping my head around this, so I'm going conservative on the numbers.

The harmful effects to kids is an endless list including but not limited to: lack of social skills, depression, poor sleep habits, obesity, warped sense of reality, stress, isolation, constant distraction, shortened attention span, lack of social and sexual boundaries, and on and on and on....

Of course my favorite part is when you consider kids are in school 7 hours a day. If they spend 8 hours with the screen sitter, that's 15 hours of their day. A 12 year old should sleep for 10 hours a day. And that puts us at a 25 hour day, which we all wish we had. Upon further review, the 12 year old isn't getting any exercise so his body doesn't need typical rest, and requires less sleep. So it's all good. Let's hear it for obese America!

Every article you will read acknowledges that there is a lot of good on the internet, and kids must have it to do their homework and other necessary activities. But you can also read statistics on the amount of time kids spend on intellectual activities versus non-productive activities, and it ain't pretty.

When you were a kid, you played with friends more, engaged in more activities and sports. You skinned your knee more, engaged in actual verbal conversations with peers and adults more plus the bike rack at your elementary school had way more bikes than your kid's school.

I could not find data on special needs kids and screen time, but I'm telling you, it's worse. Handicapped kids are famous for getting dropped off by the small bus after school and neighbors don't see them again until that same bus pulls up the following morning. They spend a lot of time inside and online.

The television has long been the best baby sitter for when parents need a break. Special needs kids are difficult in many ways and very entertained by the screen sitter. How easy is it to give a kid an iPad or a tablet and get some projects done or put your feet up for a bit. All these screens, whether in the palm of your hand or projected on the wall are the number one killer of original thought, imagination, growth, and creating real life moments.

Challenge: Seriously commit to avoid what is an epic problem in society and the special needs community. Decide now to slash the Screen Sitter! She doesn't love your child. Take whatever steps you need. Commit and don't get lazy. There are plenty of helps that are easy to find, like the site I listed above. Chances are you already know about all of this and have plans to nip it in the bud. Maybe you did already. And perhaps then you got lazy. For what it's worth, here is the Daynes family Screen Sitter Slasher Program.

73

1. No electronics of any kind in bedrooms. A bedroom with internet and or TV is a teenage wasteland.

2. Filters on all devices. Chances are you have a decent one on your router already. You can control content and time for each device. For example, Wifi for my 14 year-old's phone shuts off at 8:00PM.

3. Phones, tablets, and devices are to be at the charging station (by front door) unless permission is granted. If they want to text friends, they can do it at the charging station.

4. Have computers, TV, all in one central gathering place like the living room.

5. Electronics are allowed after homework and jobs are done and an hour of outside play time.

6. Limit two hours a day of electronics. When we grant exceptions it's usually a family movie or playing something with someone, never alone.

7. One week every 6 months without any electronics.

Whoa! Am I insane! And it's gets worse. Both Robin and I do number 7. Granted, it's usually a POG or family getaway where I don't have work related emails and correspondence. We use the phone only as a phone. Imagine that! You've got to lead on this. Can't ask your kids to do something you can't do yourself. You can tell a lot of those rules are to avoid zombie-ness and porn. Kids who have a tablet in their room can go hours and not realize they are slowly turning into zombies. Kids can find porn easily. Overlooking it only promotes it. You don't want that monstrosity and addiction in your home. Slash the screen sitter!

Create the Moments

"You can't recover the fumble if you're not on the field."

I heard or read that somewhere, and for the life of me, can't figure out who said it.
Rick

When Tyler was young and having all kinds of issues, we signed him up for indoor soccer. He was excited to be part of a team and playing a sport with a real uniform. But his style of play wasn't welcomed in the league. He was a slow kid and when others ran past him, he couldn't help but grab them a little to slow them down. It was difficult for him but he really tried to play by the rules. Nevertheless, there were too many disgruntled parents in the league who logged complaints against our 4 year old and Tyler was booted out of the league.

A year later, we tried it again with the same results. Every game had at least one questionable to bad incident. We dealt with rude parents, opposing coaches who forgot they were coaching 5 year-olds, and we were embarrassed. We often wondered why we did things like this. Why we went through the effort to sign him up in things where he might fail. We were told he doesn't belong with normal kids. So why were we putting ourselves through this? And why are we still doing it today?

Every now and then there are those shining moments like the Karate Kid story. And we talk about these moments and build them up. As we built moment upon moment we started to see real growth. Tyler is now 12 years old and is about to enter his fifth season of little league baseball. It's still a stressful situation where we need to find that coach who can deal with him. But Ty loves it and it's been an integral part of his life. He's grown dramatically with it and he's actually become pretty good.

Every year Ty asks to be in the school talent show. I'm embarrassed to say that every year I do my best to make that idea go away. That's a serious stretch where I know he's going to be embarrassed. Or maybe we're the ones who will be embarrassed. Last

75

year I repented and signed him up. We figured out a talent, worked hard on it. It was a royal pain in the butt for me. But, in the end, another miracle occurred and he hit it out of the park in front of the entire school!

In these sports, programs and activities we throw our kids into, you experience these days of turmoil and pandemonium. But then you get to witness miracles. Actual miracles! How many people get to see miracles? You also get to meet the awesome people of the world. The parents who seek out your kid and tell him how incredible his talent is. Those coaches who can turn a strike-out into a learning moment and a double into a homerun. Teachers who love, and neighbors who will give a compliment. The hundreds of moments, both big and small, both good and bad, these are the building blocks of life.

A couple years ago we were invited to an adult only holiday party. On the night of the event, I asked my friend if he and his wife were going. He replied that he wanted to but they didn't have anyone to watch their son. It's difficult to find someone to watch their boy as he has... Well, I don't know what he has. But he can't talk, can't move much, and spends everyday in bed or in his wheel chair. Pretty severely handicapped kid.

I told him to get that kid in his chair and bring him. And then I could see that moment we all go through. He's apprehensive what people will think. There are not supposed to be any kids there and he's thinking if it's worth it. He wanted to stay at home in his comfort zone and not risk whatever might happen. I said, "Look, you need to come and bring David. Let people interact with him and you for that matter. Let the awesome people meet him and love this kid and you guys. No one is going to judge anyone."

The evening was a complete success. I love my friends for coming when it would have been so easy to sit home. It's so easy to let kids become reclusive and parents homebodies. You must decide now if you are going to take easy street and stay at home with the screen sitter. Or are you going to be active, unafraid of what people might think or say, and willing to get out there.

I'm not saying run yourself ragged. There are limits to everything and only you know your limit and that of your child and family. If you don't know your limits, then get out there and test them! Take some shots! And speaking of shots, take pics and video everywhere you go. Record those memories! They are invaluable. See POG chapter for more on this.

Be dedicated to creating special moments for your family! Take advantage of anything you can, large or small. Take advantage of services for your child. Take advantage of where you live, the people you know, and anything to broaden your situation. Get creative! Live in the moment! Live now! Go camping, join a club, take a chance. Nothing ventured, nothing gained.

Savor the Moments

Parents of special needs kids know greater joy because they have had greater sorrow. They ride the rollercoaster, visiting both ends of the spectrum. Their lows are Death Valley but their highs ride the peaks of the Sierras. They are the miracle makers.

Special needs parents learn to slow down the moment and bottle those stories. I've got hundreds of them myself. Building a sandcastle, playing in the rain, making Mommy breakfast in bed both with and without spilling something on her, a thousand little triumphs, a hundred miracles, all stored in the memory vaults. Those vaults are for the most part in my head, but a few have made it to paper or the computer where they should all be!

Special needs parents take nothing for granted. The time your son walked out of the bathroom and no one had to tell him to wash his hands! Priceless! The words or signs your daughter learned to communicate. Awesome! The new expression on your boy's face. We savor the moments!

Many parents have countless celebrations while others don't know when the next good moment will come. But when it does, they internalize it and make it priceless. Remember, life is defined by moments. No matter how large or small, you can slow them down and make it a party. When you do, you produce a culture that promotes it again and again.

The Rundown

Create, Record, Enlarge, Savor, Repeat

1. Special memories are there for the taking.

2. Watch and Learn. Make decisions before you get there.

3. Epidemic. Slash the screen sitters! Too much electronics.

4. Create the moments. Get out there and make it happen miracle maker!

5. Savor the Moments.

    A. Parents of special needs kids know greater happiness.

    B. Record the memories.

    C. Enlarge the moments! Build upon them.

    D. Do it again.

IEP
(Individualized Education Plan/Program)

Dusty Bottoms: "Time for plan B. Plan A was to break into El Guapo's fortress."

Carmen: "And that you have done, now what? "

Dusty Bottoms: "Well we really don't have a plan B. We didn't expect for the first plan to work. Sometimes you can overplan these things."
Three Amigos.

The "Thing"
(wife warning)

"I've been thinking about this, Mr. Hand. If I'm here and you're here, doesn't that make it our time? Certainly there's nothing wrong with a little feast on our time."
Jeff Spicoli Fast Times at Ridgemont High

I have written this book with your time being of the upmost importance. I am only including subjects you need to spend time on. If it isn't in this book, don't worry too much or at all. School functions, plays, sports, anything important to your kid, is always good to support, of course. That parent teacher conference you missed? No big deal, you already laid the groundwork there and have a good ongoing relationship with the teacher. Your wife can handle that. PTA, Special Education Conference, awards meetings, fundraisers, a million parties and activities supporting Autism and Aspergers and Down Syndrome and MS, and who knows what on every spectrum. All that stuff is good, but NOT MANDATORY.

Don't ditch work for all these shindigs. Going to Speech, PT (Physical Therapy), OT (Occupational Therapy), and other services with your kid are always good, but not a high priority for you, <u>unless your wife tells you it is</u>. Let's not kid ourselves here. There are events we go to that have no bearing on anyone or anything except to support our wives and marriage. A man's got to do what a man's got to do. And sometimes you need to suck it up, take one for the team, and just go because she tells you to go.

There are several programs for parents and families, which teach everyone how to deal with your special child. There are no short-ages of six-week courses here or a one night seminar there. I have done my share of them. Some were worth it and others not. Here's how I judge if I have spent time wisely on a class. Say, when I walk out of a one-hour seminar on anything Autism. I spent one hour in there plus an hour of transportation getting there and back. I've invested two total hours in this function to somehow better myself or my family. If I would have spent those two hours with my boy at the park, giving him all my attention, what would have been more beneficial? I realize you'll have to factor in the, now benefit, and any future benefit, but you get the picture.

That's how to determine if the conference was worth it. That's the benchmark. Now, I do not claim to know everything. I've got a lot to learn. But you can imagine, using that benchmark, I attend far fewer of these events than I have in the past. My wife? Not the case. More often than not, she goes and I stay. In fact, at this very moment, Robin is at a 'thing.' Some of these classes have such elaborate names, plus there are so many of them that I cannot keep track. So I just call them the 'Thing.'

When my wife left an hour ago, I didn't say, "Honey, have fun at the teaching your kid to verbally communicate class for the Autistic that you are really going to for help with our boy with Down Syndrome." I said, "Honey, have fun at the Thing." She knows what I'm talking about.

This Thing is an eight-week course where parents meet every Wednesday night and an expert on verbal communication, "who has had amazing results," is teaching. Last week was the first week. I opted to stay home and build forts with our kids. My desire not to go was validated when Robin got home from the class. She said the teacher brought food and they went around the room and talked about their kids and ate. They did not start the class. It was purely a get-to-know-you night.

You can only imagine how I would have done that first week. I would have put on a smile and done my best, but inside I would have been boiling. You mean I paid for a sitter to watch my kids so I could drive down here and listen to all these strangers give me their life story? Seriously? We are not having a lesson tonight? We are just here to get to know each other? We are busy people and if we make the sacrifice to get here, there better be some substance or benefit to coming other than food.

Robin on the other hand is fine with that. Chicks love that stuff! They eat it up, literally. The talking, crying, getting your emotions out, is great for her. She gets the chance to rub shoulders with women battling just like she is and feels support. Does that sound familiar? Welcome to the special needs branch of the Pick-A-Littles! They are dialed in and the source of cool benefits (benes) and more and more 'Things' (seminars). Like the school version, we love the disability Pick-A-Littles. We wouldn't know about 'getting half off at Disney Land', several cool parties, and our favorite 'Things' without them! I've become a pretty good Pick-A-Little myself! When I meet someone who has a kid with a disability, I love to share my top benes. Unfortunately special needs Pick-A-Littles are also the source of 'Things' that are not worth taking time away from family.

I don't know if this current verbal communication Thing will be worth it, but in the first gathering, which I did not attend, I've spotted two major deterrents that validate my absence. One, there were no nuggets or meat (lesson). Nothing was presented that I could take home and improve my life. Two, they had a sign-up sheet go around for food assignments. Each week someone is bringing food. *What is with the food?* Why do so many of these meetings come with food? Don't get me wrong, I'm a huge fan of food! No one loves food more than me. Having food at 'Things' draws guys like me out. But the stress it will bring to my wife and consequently our entire house for her one night of bringing food, will not be worth it.

But that's what they do. Doesn't matter if everyone is fat and already had dinner that night, they are bringing food. And each week, some poor lady is going to stress about what food to bring, how much, how to serve, how to transport, what it will cost, any food allergies, will it be as good as Cindy's, what if no one likes it, and gas it might cause during class. For me, I'm staying home again and roll around on the floor with my boys. I'll be at home for the entire eight week course. I'll have saved a few hundred dollars in babysitting fees, invested invaluable time with my rug rats, and Robin can teach me any positive lessons that will change our lives. Everyone wins!

I don't mean to make fun of 'Things.' Actually, that's not true. I love to make fun of 'Things.' But for the record, 'Things' rock! Well, most 'Things' rock. They are usually free and are awesome sources of helps and tools that change people's lives! Miracles happen in these classes and seminars. I do recommend you attend whatever you feel might be beneficial to your child, family, or you. It's a great excuse to get out on a date too. I can't say enough about the wonderful people who put them on. All the volunteers and people and companies who donate to keep programs and benes running.

If you are new to the world of disabilities, you might be tempted to jump into every 'Thing' you can find. Your wife will. Try to limit yourself. If you live in a large city, there might be endless studies and programs and seminars and 'Things.' Next thing you know you've spread yourself too thin and neglected what really matters. Remember to use the benchmark. Will your time be better spent one-on-one with your kid or getting the babysitter and going to the 'Thing?' If you choose to stay, you must spend the time interacting with your kid! Don't weasel out and let him or you watch TV.

IEP: Attendance Mandatory

I will tell you one meeting you won't need to consider the benchmark for, and that is the IEP. The IEP meeting is NOT A THING. It is absolutely essential that you attend and participate. If an IEP is scheduled when you are out of town, you reschedule one of them. If you have to miss work, you do it. You move heaven and earth to be there. UNDER NO CIRCUMSTANCES DO YOU LET AN IEP HAPPEN WITHOUT YOU. This is the Super Bowl, the

World Series, the last episode of Seinfeld, Grand Poobah of meetings. Am I being clear on this? Good, because it's getting its own section.

Record

"Check. Check 1. Sibilance. Sibilance. Check. Check 2. Sibilance. Sibilance."
Barry (Tom Hanks) Saturday Night Live sketch with Aerosmith and Waynes World.

Audio record every meeting. It does not matter if every big wig in the district is there. It does not matter if there is a full blown law suit in progress. It does not matter if you have an IEP once a year and it's a cream puff meeting. It does not matter if the same thing happens every year and all is hunky dori. YOU MUST RECORD EVERY IEP.

BY LAW YOU MUST GIVE THE DISTRICT 24 HOUR WRITTEN NOTICE THAT YOU WILL RECORD THE IEP MEETING. DO NOT FORGET. But if you forget, record anyway.

The reasons for recording are as follows:

1. It tells the IEP team that you are serious.

2. You have a record of everything that went on, everything said, everything implied, during that meeting. You may think that everyone on your IEP team is Mother Teresa and nothing will ever disrupt the flow of your child's education. But stuff happens even to the best people on earth. There are a million variables in your child's life and YOU NEVER KNOW if or when you are going to need something that was said during your meeting.

3. It's a layup. I'm not asking you to walk an elephant into the room. Your cell has a digital recording app as well as your lap top and who knows what else. Make sure you know how to work it. See that the device is charged and take a charge cord just in case the meeting goes longer than your charge. Easy peasy lemon squeezy.

4. Why not? No downside. No one is going to be offended that you want to record. They should expect you will.

Food

"They always got food with them. We eat to live - these guys live to eat! Let me show you what I'm talking about! The human mouth is called a 'piehole', the human being is called a 'couch potato'. That is a device to summon food. That is one of the many voices of food. That is the portal for the passing of food. That is one of the many food transportation vehicles. Humans bring the food, take the food, ship the food, they drive food, they wear the food! That gets the food hot! That keeps the food cold! That... I'm not sure what that is. Well, what do you know? FOOD! That is the altar where they WORSHIP food! That's what they eat when they've eaten TOO MUCH food! That gets rid of the guilt so they can eat MORE FOOD! FOOD! FOOD! FOOD! FOOD! FOOOOOD!" RJ (Bruce Willis) Over the Hedge.

Previously, I have mentioned my disdain for the humans who assign food at meetings. This should not be confused with disdain for having food at meetings. I love food at meetings. I just don't like when my wife is the one in charge of bringing the food. In that case, the rule is, it's far better not to have food at all, if your wife is assigned to bring it. Now, having said that, please ask your wife nicely to bring food to this meeting. This is the exception to the rule. This is the one meeting when you want to bring food.

IEP meetings can be uncomfortable to say the least. Rolling into the meeting bearing gifts is a great way to start things off. If any member of the team, including yourself, arrives with a negative attitude or even thinks things are going to get sticky, a gesture of thanksgiving and good will is the best way to instantly diffuse potential hostility.

And what is better than food? It's easy. It tells your team that you care and are thankful to them for their efforts. It's a present! It starts the meeting off by you thanking everyone and in turn they get a chance to thank you. Thanking you is not the point. It's that everyone is thanking someone. They talk about the treat. They acknowledge the thoughtful gift. And they say those magic words that everyone loves to say and hear. Thank you! There is something about being thankful that really softens people, makes them more pleasant, and opens them up.

For IEP meetings held in the morning, Robin will bring something like bagels and cream cheese. For less formal morning meetings, donuts do fine. For some reason, we usually have an IEP or two before Winter Break. We start the meeting off by Robin rolling out a spread of scrumptious Christmas cookies and sweets. Then she gives an individually wrapped Christmas or Hanukah present to everyone. It's usually these cookies called Peppermint Jo Jo's from Trader Joes. It's a cookie that looks like an Oreo, but has a peppermint flavor. My mouth is watering just thinking about them! Let your wife get creative on this food thing. You can get it done also, but it won't be as good as when your wife does it. Plus women love that stuff. Robin usually adds some decoration and it always looks great. Since most of the room is filled with women, they love the presentation. You want these people on your side. They want you on their side as well. Food is just a little way to bring everyone together.

Attire

"Come on Cinderella, we got to get you ready for the ball!" Dumb and Dumber

Ah yes, what to wear? Hmm... How about brushing off that old suit, my man! Because you are wearing it! Yes, I am serious. I know it's a more casual world and not as many people wear a tie these days. Don't fight the fashion! When you walk into that room and you are bearing gifts and wearing a suit! It is game on game over! I'm not into clichés, but first impressions ARE EVERYTHING.

Putting on the formal garb tells your team again that, once again, you are serious. They may think you dress like that everyday when you go to the office. They may know that's not the case and you are simply dressed up for this meeting. Either way they think, it's all good. Dress to impress! And tell your wife to do the same.

Look, I'm not a formal guy. I'm from San Diego. I went to college in Hawaii. My first job out of College was in Key West Florida. I know casual. I don't even like wearing shoes. But I dawn the suit for the IEP with little exception. Here's the dress standard:

First IEP meeting or any IEP meeting with a new team calls for mandatory suit gear. All other meetings with the same IEP team for the next 18 months you must wear a tie. After 18 months you can ditch the tie if and only if the meetings are becoming more casual and routine. You may ditch the tie, but nothing else. You still need to look good for every IEP. Keep the nice button down shirt, pants, shoes, etc. If serious decisions are being made or outside people are brought in, consider bringing the tie and/or suit back.

Basics

I am stealing the following paragraph from the chapter titled "Tyler's Year." It describes my first experience with an IEP meeting.

Preparing for our first IEP (Individual Education Plan) meeting was no small task. I drove 45 minutes to an office where I met with an IEP Specialist who trained me in the fine art of the IEP meeting. First thing she did was hand me a book as thick as the Bible and tell me I needed to read and know it. It contains all the current laws and regulations. And good news! A new addition comes out every year! Can't wait for next year's addition! Yeah! Not really. Then we talked about what to do. What to say. What's it like. Who is there. Who speaks. Who conducts. What to bring. Whether or not we need an advocate. What to wear. How to act. When to sign forms. Who will help us review. And on, and on, and on.

Since that first IEP meeting I've put in a lot more time on this subject. However, I've learned more from being there and talking to others about their experiences, than reading that massive book. You'll learn that way too. But for now, consider this basic advice you're getting from a friend (me).

The IEP is a legal document that states exactly what services your child gets. It puts him or her in a classification for getting these services. I believe there are currently 13 classifications encompassing everything from blind to brain injury. The IEP could include behavior plans, one-on-one aides, time spent in classes, services, and goals. Every kid is different and that is why the plan is custom made to each child. Modifications and updates to the plan occur as needed and not necessarily in an IEP meeting.

The meeting is attended by all the major players in your child's education. The teacher, program specialist, psychologist, therapists and others could be there. I have attended meetings when there were fewer people in attendance and I've attended meeting where we needed a large room to accommodate all the district officials, attorneys, outside specialists, etc. That was a fun one.

We have gone through eight principals with our kids who have IEP's. Some principals go all the time and some go none of the time. If you like your principal, do what you can to get him or her there. If you don't like your principal, avoid action to keep him out of the meeting. I have seen that back fire.

These meetings generally last an hour but can go forever. Always plan on your IEP meeting going three times longer than you think. One hour IEP? Block out three hours. Here's why. They quite often do go long though not three times as long. Following your meeting, there might be a teacher or Principal or someone who generally cares about your kid who wants to talk. These conversations are invaluable and you should not hurry them. Also, a little down time with your wife after the meeting can be just what the doctor or-dered. Who knows, if there's time, you can go grab lunch together and talk about how the IEP was. So tell that babysitter and work that it's a 3 hour meeting.

Don't Get Drilled

"When the wave breaks here, don't be there or you're gona get drilled."

Turtle, The North Shore

You can see why I put huge weight on this meeting and why at-tendance is mandatory. All the decisions for your child's education are made in this meeting by these players. There is a tremendous amount of information out there on IEP's. I could write a book only on IEP's myself. Maybe I will. But I'm keeping it basic for now.

There are advocates who will go with you and experts and friends who can train you.

Ignorance is not bliss when it comes to IEP meetings. You cannot blindly trust that your team will put your child in the best situation for his success. Too many couples have gone into their IEP meetings and let their team, or someone on the team dominate the meeting and control the outcome. Nothing burns me more than an administrator who takes advantage of parents because they are ignorant. It does not happen a lot, but don't think that it cannot happen to you.

I have a good friend who was bullied into homeschooling their daughter. Homeschooling can be great, but don't go there because your school says to do it. Districts can be very good at withholding resources and information. You need to prepare. You need to do a little homework so you don't get drilled.

Resources are there for anything you need. Google can answer any question you have and there is always that monster book with every law, rule, and guideline known to the IEP world. Never sign anything until you have reviewed everything thoroughly and both you and your wife AGREE. You don't have to sign anything after the meeting. They will print out the IEP and slide it over to you with a pen.

You do not have to sign! You can sleep on it, take it to an advocate, or someone who knows what they are doing. I love my wife in these meetings. We had an IEP just last week. At the conclusion of the meeting, they printed out the document and slid it over for signatures. The meeting was concluding, people were getting ready to leave. Robin took her time reading through it. Then she mentioned three things we discussed in the meeting that she wanted included in the IEP. So she had them tear up the one in her hand and redo it. Just because people are tired and want to get out of there, do not be pressured to sign the doc and get out of there. This is your child's IEP. It is special! Make sure it's right.

Do not be afraid to find help! The IEP community of parents talk. They are in your club. They are in your corner. Seek out the Pick-A-Littles. They will help. Advocates can be free to expensive. Lawyers can be free to expensive. Yes, I said it. Free legal advice. Free attorneys who go into IEP meetings with you. There are colleges with law students hungry for IEP experience and they will sometimes come for free.

There are law firms you can go to that will review your case for free. If they feel you have a case they will represent you for free. I know a lawyer who told me he has never billed his client. When I asked how he got paid, he explained. It's all about free and appropriate education. If we can prove the district has not done their job, it's on them. We see to it the child gets the proper placement and services and then we bill the district. After all, they are the ones who screwed up. Some attorneys will tell you your case isn't solid and charge you. Others might work for cheap. They are all different. My point is, don't be timid in looking for help whether you are rich or poor. Help is out there.

I'll never forget the first IEP meeting we took our lawyer to. She sat silent for about 20 minutes. Then she asked a question. She did not agree with the response she got and confidently retorted, "A judge wouldn't see it that way." There was a deafening silence for a minute as everyone in that room knew she was right. Just that one statement was the turning point in Tyler's education. It let the district know that we were serious and if they wanted to screw around with our child that we would fight. I sincerely hope you never have to deal with horrible placement and an IEP team who cannot get it right. But if you do, be confident in standing up for your rights.

Above all else know this! You and your wife are by far the most important players in the IEP. You are Captains of that team. No one in that room knows YOUR child like you and your wife do. You are the foremost authority no matter how much schooling, degrees, experience, expertise anyone in that room has. There could be 10,000 IEP possibilities between everyone in the room. Even though it's your first, you have more knowledge on the subject (kid), say in the matter, and overall power than anyone. Use it to your advantage and don't let it override what and who you are really there for.

Plan

"Everyone has a plan 'till they get punched in the mouth." Mike Tyson

You and your wife should have a plan. Schedule a time to discuss what you like and dislike about your child's education and really his or her entire life. Generally, this should be a brief meeting because in your day-to-day life, you are already aware of what's working and what's not. This is that time when the two of you talk about subjects that will be discussed and decisions that may or may not be made. It's perfectly fine to go into your IEP lacking answers. IEP's are a team effort and you'll be able to draw from everyone in the room if needed.

This is a brief meeting between you and your wife to make sure the two of you are on the same page. This is not the time to dissect every incident and mill around every negative behavior of your child or anyone. If you absolutely have to hash things out about something beneficial to the IEP, then do it. But focus around how your last IEP was. What went well and what didn't. What did you say last time that you regret now. What came out of your mouth that perhaps should have come out of your wife's and vice versa or not at all.

PLAN WITH YOUR OBJECTIVES IN MIND. See objectives down the page a bit. Go through your pre-game checklist, also listed down the page. Between you and your wife, you should have a good idea of what will be said and what will happen. Make sure you know where your wife stands and that she knows where you stand. There should be no surprises in the meeting especially between the two of you.

However! I am not in the habit of telling people to do what Mike Tyson suggests. But referencing his quote above, a punch in the mouth can come in many forms: The district informing you that your child doesn't qualify for something she badly needs. There is no room in a certain program you had your heart set on. The one-on-one aide is being pulled. An off colored, offensive, or insulting remark directed at you or worse, your wife. If the punch in the mouth arrives in any of it's forms, do not freak out. Keep your cool, stick to the plan. Cooler heads will prevail.

MOST IMPORTANT! BE A TEAM! It does not matter if you and your wife are currently in the worst fight of your marriage. It doesn't matter if you are divorced and you and your ex hate each other to no end. For the sake of your child, you must stand as one during this meeting. Any subtle dissention or resentment between the two of you will be picked up by your team. There is only one person that matters during this meeting. It isn't you. It isn't your wife. It isn't anyone in the room. It's that little person who calls you Daddy. Remember that! Be one! Be a team!

Pre-Game

1. Arrive 15 minutes early? Check. If you are not 15 minutes early to your IEP, then you are late.

2. Babysitter and kids taken care of for the next three hours? Check

3. Work put on hold for the next three hours? Check

4. Digital recording device charged and ready? Check

5. Charge cord for the recording device? Check

6. Notebook and paper? Check

7. Any and all materials you might need? Check. Usually a copy of assessments, assignments, past IEP's and other documents are emailed around prior to the meeting. Sometimes bringing in homework or something to illustrate your point is good.

8. Food? Check

9. Gifts? Check. This is optional. Robin will give out goodies or small presents to take home before some holidays and end of the year.

10. Dressed up and feeling good? Check

11. Wife looking hotter than Papa Bear's porridge, *and you have told her so*? Check

12. Last minute discussion, if any? Check

13. Prayer? Check. My wife and I both believe in God. It would be impossible not to given the things we've been through. So we like to embrace and have a word of prayer before we go in. It's a good team building exercise. I suppose you could do a cheer or two-man pyramid if you want.

14. Last minute words of encouragement? Check

Game On

This is basic people skills, but I'm going to say it anyway because some of you need to hear it. As you and your bride walk in, *hand in hand,* be sure to put on a smile and greet everyone with a firm handshake. Pass out the goodies and get to know everyone. If you already know everyone, a little small talk or catch up is always valued. If you can bring up conversation other than what you are there for, do it. Ask the Principal about their last assembly or the Speech Therapist how her golf game is, anything. Show some interest in others. It helps break the group down and makes everyone more comfortable. Pull your wife's chair out for her and treat her like a queen. Sit close to her and be happy you get to hang out with your wife. Remember, you are a team.

These meetings can get stuffy, so keep it light. A good book for everyone and especially those who need to brush up on their people skills is "How to Win Friends and Influence People" by Dale Carnegie. It was written dog years ago and is still the best people person book around. I'm not going to get into basic people skills, but try to keep everyone in a good mood. Be yourself. Don't be intimidated. If you're goofy and a little funny, let it out.

Most of the meeting is mandatory garb they have to go over. Lots of formal stuff that will bore you to tears. Feel free to ask questions any time about anything but be weary of slowing down the meeting. Some stuff you need to get through so you can get down to the nitty-gritty. Don't speak a lot but ask questions anytime. Often times, discussions and resolutions come as a result of your questions. Even additions to the IEP come simply from observing and asking questions. "What was little Susie's reaction when you did that... How does he do in this situation....Have you done this with him...Would you recommend we do that at home to help....How do you think we can improve this or that...Do you think she would benefit from... Can you steer us in the right direction regarding that? Ask questions!

Remember, you and the misses are the most important people in the room. Don't let anything slide that is wrong. There will be subject matter in the grey areas. Things you are not sure of. A lot of decisions can be educated guesses or a leap of faith. Will little Johnny benefit from this service? He didn't last week, but maybe now? Don't be afraid to lean on your team! Don't discount anyone, even if they look funny or rub you the wrong way. You will get a good feel for your team. Some people you will value more than others. And you will feel like some care more than others.

At some point and maybe several points during the meeting, you need to offer support. Such as, "What can we at home do to help Jr. in this area or reach these goals?" Remember, you are one big happy team. What you do at home should support what happens at school. You would be surprised how many teachers are reluctant to come out and ask you to do exercises or assignments they feel will make your kid a better person.

Take the meeting in stride, stick to the plan, and don't sign anything at the end unless you are confident in what it reads. You can add or amend things later, and you can call another IEP meeting. There is no shame in telling your team you would like to sleep on it before signing the IEP.

Hopefully you have a productive meeting and are able to address and facilitate the needs of your child. Most of the IEP meetings I have attended have been very positive experiences even when there are serious disagreements within the team. At the end of every meeting you need to send a little love. Yes, I know you already did this at the beginning when you showed up with the grub. But you've got to do it one more time.

93

You just went through an IEP meeting. It could have been grueling or easy. Doesn't matter. People are tired, goals have been set, and things written into your kid's IEP probably changed. I usually say something like this, "Hey, real quick, I know we're ending here. I'd just like to tell everyone how grateful Robin and I are for all of you. We live with little Ricky so we know he is not the easiest kid to work with. We really appreciate your efforts. Also, dealing with us and these IEP meetings are not on your top 10 list of fun things to do. So thanks for being patient with us. We are always open to communication and suggestions."

Now, let's say the meeting isn't going according to plan and Mike Tyson punches you in the mouth, so to speak. And about that. We need to establish one important fact. I read all the time about parents and their horrible experiences in IEP meetings. There are even lists of worst things said and worst experiences on line, just ready for anyone to read. Look at what this principal said. Can you believe a school counselor said this?

But let's be honest here. You are not going to find rebuttals from those administrators. Nor will you find much on worst parents in an IEP meeting. That's because a parent can publish what they want without repercussions and an employee of the school district cannot. Can you imagine the stories these IEP facilitators could tell? They would be outrageous. But you'll never hear it, because they would be looking for a job the next day.

Who is the most emotional when discussing little Maggie? Who has the most invested? Who wants to give her the world? Who loves her the most? And who is most likely to be offended if things don't go their way? That's right, the parents. More specifically, your wife is likely more emotional than you and will break down or storm out of the room first. Depending on your wits, you could be right behind her. My point being your wife or you is most likely the culprit when it comes to the first one throwing a punch, figuratively speaking of course.

Please put yourself in the shoes of the teachers or specialists sitting across from you. Yes, there is the occasional insensitive jerk or Mrs. My Way or the Highway. But more often than not, you might

94

want to take a look in the mirror if things get out of hand. And if they do, it is less likely you are going to be giving little Magie the best chance for success. If mistakes are made by anyone in the meeting, there are other ways of getting things done. When the meeting ends, DO NOT SIGN ANYTHING. Take a copy of the IEP home, cool off, and reach out. There are people waiting to help.

Objectives

What you are really there for is quite simple. Everyone on your IEP team should have the same objective. And that is to <u>write the best possible Individualized Education Plan for your child</u>. Unfortunately, egos, impatience, and being easily offended can get in the way. You cram all these people in a room together and you have a mixture of personalities that may or may not get along. Your team already knows each other. They could be at each other's throats on a totally different matter. You don't want that or any ill feeling toward anyone trailing into your room. They are professionals, but are human. You don't know if they've all gone through a brutal four hour IEP the day before and are sick of hearing each other spout off about things they have no business saying.

Here are three subsequent objectives to keep in mind from the moment you begin planning until you leave the meeting. These will help you avoid any shenanigans and write the best possible IEP.

Objective #1

Keep the temperature in the room at a cool 68.5 degrees. You get what I'm saying here? The mood or feeling in the room must be kept at the optimal temperature conducive to figure out the best plan for your child. Set the thermostat at positive, polite, and amusing. You do this by being yourself, asking questions, cracking a joke or two, bringing goodies, and smiling! And most important, you took control of the situation when you knew it was a sensitive area for your wife.

Objective #2

Send the message that you are an involved Dad. You genuinely care and are serious as a heart attack over the well-being and education of your child. You did this by being on time. You dressed up, stayed on top of the meeting, and brought the treats! You also gave them written notice you would record the meeting and did so. You were prepared and they got the message loud and clear.

Objective #3

Let them know that you and your wife are a loving and inseparable team dedicated to your child. You did this by prepping, praying, and planning together. You encouraged and complemented her before walking in, hand in hand. You were a gentleman and treated your wife life a queen. You openly complimented her about what an awesome mom she is and how she works wonders with your kid. If you had a disagreement or question between the two of you, you wrote a note or whispered in her ear. It's not the end of the world if the team knows Mr. and Mrs. Daynes don't agree. You can invite a discussion to help the two of you resolve differences. Just do it politely and respectfully. You can also call for a break if the two of you need to discuss something. Also, you both look spectacular. More so your wife than you, but that's usually how it goes.

The Run Down

1. The Thing (any seminar, party, program, fundraiser, meeting, etc.). If it's more beneficial to spend the same amount of time with your child, than at the thing, bail the Thing.

2. IEP Attendance is mandatory.

3. Record all IEP meetings.

4. Bring food.

5. Wear a suit.

6. There are IEP basics and then there are a whole lot more.

7. Have a plan. Plan with your wife and with your objectives in mind.

8. Go through your pre-game checklist.

9. Game on. Keep it real.

10. Objective: Write the best possible IEP for your child

   A. Keep it cool!

   B. You are an involved Dad!

   C. You and your lady are a team!

Part II
Mama Bear

Holy Matrimony

"Married men live longer than single men. But married men are a lot more willing to die."

Johnny Carson

On a gorgeous summer day in which the sun shone bright and a light sea breeze aided in drying tears of joy, Michelle and Scott were married. It was the perfect day for the perfect couple. Full of life and potential, they had the world with all of its adventures and romance before them. The celebration went late into the night before the couple checked into their honeymoon villa overlooking the tranquil cove.

Late the next morning Scott and Michelle Rogers wrapped in terry cloth robes enjoyed brunch on their veranda. They beamed into each other's eyes, and laughed at the weekend's surreal events. Michelle welled up as they discussed family and dear friends who sacrificed so much for them. They vowed to never forget these dear people who traveled great distances to be at their wedding.

They deserved each other, as well as this moment. They savored its sweetness long past their honeymoon and years into their marriage. They were prepared for the trials and joys of married life as much as anyone. They were smart and understood marriage wouldn't always come so easy.

Michelle gave birth to a beautiful boy expanding their family and giving them joy they didn't know was possible. A precious little girl came next, followed by the dog and experiments with a few more pets. Responsibilities increased, but the Rogers worked hard at their life and enjoyed the fruit of their labors. 15 years into their marriage, the Rogers were involved in family, schools, community, church, and careers.

Michelle's friend Carla brought her daughter over for a play date one afternoon. As she entered the house she couldn't help but notice how clean and tidy Michelle kept things. She certainly had it all together and complimented her on how perfect everyone looked in the family portrait hanging flawlessly over the living room mantel. Michelle thanked Carla for the compliment and then said, "Carla, Scott moved out a few days ago. We've separated." Carla reacted as any friend would. After being shocked by the news, Carla hugged Michelle and tried to give support and comfort to her friend.

An hour later Carla left with a new realization than the one she walked in with. Although the Rogers were perfect on the outside, it was an entirely different story on the inside. Another hour later you could almost see the neighborhood phone lines turning red, burning as new gossip spread like fire in a wind storm.

Most friends remained neutral and supportive. "They just didn't love each other... They agreed to stay together until their kids were gone, but it was just too much... Counseling didn't work... They lived more like roommates for longer than you think."

Others took sides. "She was a control freak. It was her way or the highway... He worked hard and loved them all so much and got no support from her... When Scott had his salary cut, she couldn't break her spending habits and sent them into serious debt... She kept screaming at him to make more money... Imagine coming home after working hard all day and getting nagged at all night... Hinting for sex only made things worse. Who could live like that?"

"He was addicted to everything on line. Video gaming, gambling, pornography, it drove his wife away... Hours spent on his phone, computer, and all the latest gadgets just to satisfy his obsessions... It entirely consumed him. Someone said he became a monster... Michelle suspected he was cheating on her when he began coming home later, and business trips ran longer... Of course he insisted on buying that house, which put them in a financial hole they'll never crawl out of.

My dad often tells the story of a wedding he went to in which the pastor performing the ceremony had some untraditional words for the couple. He looked over the audience and then at this young couple standing at the altar and said, "The day will come when you will no longer want to be married to this person." The chapel instantly drained of all sound. He paused to let that statement sink in.

The pastor went on to turn that negative phase into a positive message of course. But what a powerful message that sent to the newlyweds and everyone in attendance. Although happy as clams at the moment, there would come a time when they would no longer want to be married to that person. I imagine every married couple in the room thought about that statement. Some may have thought that was not the right venue for a statement like that. But no one could disagree.

83%

C-3PO: "Sir, the possibility of successfully navigating an asteroid field is approximately 3720 to 1."

Han Solo: "Never tell me the odds "

Star Wars

Our Tyler has a really cool case worker whom we enjoy. She once told us the divorce rate of parents with a special needs kid was 83%. In college I spent a lot of time studying statistics and historical accounts that differ from one another. I learned that anything can be manipulated or just plain falsely documented. For example, not long ago there was no shortage of news outlets reporting the divorce rate of parents with an autistic child was as high as 80%. That ended up being a false report.[4] Why the exaggeration? Why do false reports get traction and grow? To this day I have a hard time believing a lot of statistics and studies without some investigation. I attempted to look up the 83% study, and could not find it. I did find a lot of other case studies about the traditional notion that half of all marriages end in divorce as well as factors into divorce and all sorts of stuff. I am not going to get into those here.

You may have looked at it the other way around. That is, 'your chances of a successful marriage are only 17%.' Wholly smokes! That sounds even worse! So why am I talking about it if I can not prove it? I'm a skeptic and not sure an accurate statistic could exist. There would be so many variables. What period of time? What age group? Can you lump all disabilities into one group? Previously divorced? Etc.

The reason I'm addressing it is because when she told me that statistic, there was no doubt in my mind that it was true! Why did I feel that way? Well, at that time, life was not sweet and I felt like that statistic. It instantly resonated with me because I did not want to be married to my wife anymore.

It wasn't because of my kid. I was up for the challenge of raising a disabled kid. I accepted that challenge. But I did not know the effect a disabled kid would have on my wife. I did not sign up for that. I was not up for dealing with this stranger who vaguely resembled the woman I married.

Beware Mama Bear

"If I didn't have my films as an outlet for all the different sides of me, I would probably be locked up."

Angelina Jolie

One of the changes your wife will experience is the Mama Bear phase. It really needs no explanation. We have all seen the entertaining videos of mama bears and the tenacious way they protect their young. Cubs are always getting into trouble and mama bear is relentless in her efforts to rescue and keep them in line.

Mama Bear has one problem though. In all those videos of mama bear attacking the mountain lion, or anything that threatens her cubs, did you ever see papa bear? Hundreds of videos of mama bear and her cubs and you never see papa bear. Where is papa bear? Wouldn't it be easier to protect the cubs with a mama and a papa? Wouldn't mama bear get more sleep and be happier with papa bear taking a shift or two so she could relax and get that beehive project done? There is a papa right? She didn't make those kids on her own.

Unfortunately, papa bear only exists in *Goldie Locks and the Three Bears*. He isn't around because, well, lets just say there are a lot of bad dads in the animal kingdom and papa bear is at the top of the list. So mama bear has developed instincts to protect, feed, and teach the cubs everything they need to know. Those mama bear instincts will manifest in your wife when her children are threatened.

When you have a child who is disabled or different, they are more susceptible to criticism and prejudice and trouble. Therefore mama bear will be out and about more than the usual mom. In fact, mama bear can be out a lot more than anyone wants. But the instinctual watching and caring and defending is constant. Thus it is difficult to shut off mama bear mode. Consequently papa bear will retreat more often to his man cave, often times with the kids.

Coach Kinsfather

"You learn more from getting your butt kicked than getting it kissed." Tom Hanks

I grew up in an athletic family. Every season we all played a sport. We watched a lot of sports and were interested in the history and drama of the games. We loved sports speeches. The head coach delivering his pre-game pep talk to the boys before the whistle sounded. Nothing made a sports movie like an emotional speech from the coach. Over the years we have made our own list of great sports speeches.

The summer before sixth grade my parents asked us about taking a family vacation two weeks before school started. This would mean my brothers and I would miss the first week of football practice. We liked football, but hated the first week of practice. So we were just fine skipping that week. Upon our return, we found out that there were so many kids my age, they had to make two teams. At the end of that first week, they took the best kids and put them on the "Pee Wee A Team." Those who didn't make the cut went to the "Pee Wee B Team." Because I was absent that first week, I didn't get a try-out and was automatically put on the B team.

Midway through the season, we had a perfect record. And it was not even close. Looking at the rest of the schedule it was clear we were good enough to complete the season without a positive number in the win column. The perfect season was inevitable.

There was one other place in the County that had enough kids to field two teams, Valencia Park (VP). Historically, VP probably has produced more football stars than anywhere else in San Diego County. Marcus Allen and Terrell Davis just to name a couple. We had already been whipped by their B team. Their A team was just like us, a perfect record, and it wasn't even close. Except our records were mirror images of each other.

On the eve of the big game between the undefeated VP "A" Team versus the defeated Grossmont LaMesa "B" Team, we took a knee and waited for Coach Kinsfather's inspirational speech. Coach Kinsfather always had good motivational words for us no matter who we were going up against. But I remember thinking to myself, what could he possibly say in this situation? Maybe dig up something from Rocky or Vince Lombardi?

He simply stood over us, looked around at everyone taking a knee and said, "Boys, I ain't gonna' lie to you. Tomorrow, you are going to get your butts kicked. So let's show up and try to make the most of it."

Friend, please think about what your wife goes through every day. Think about her schedule, the problems she takes on, the kids and people she deals with. Maybe she has an exhausting schedule running kids around all day to therapy and clinics and Things. Maybe her schedule is manageable. Maybe she works, and the two of you juggle the home and family responsibilities. Whatever the case may be, add mama bear mode to it because of something that happened to your kid at school, and you are going to get your butt kicked. Sometimes it's inevitable. You try to be the loving husband. Maybe you work around the house a little more to lighten her load. Maybe you try to get out in front of her next project. But sometimes, you might get your butt kicked, just because.

You know if you argue, you will lose. If you say the wrong thing, life could be difficult for a long time. If you say the right thing but with the wrong facial expression or tone, you will not have the option of escaping to the man cave, but will be sentenced to the doghouse. Sometimes, mama bear needs to let off some steam and kick some butt. Do everything you can to lighten her load, and be pleasant. 'Sorry,' may or may not work, because you have way overused it. Stay the course, don't get discouraged, and take your lickings. Sometimes, you are going to get your butt kicked. So just show up and try to make the most of it.

It Takes Two

I read the paper every day and the Bible every day; that way I know what both sides are up to. Zig Ziglar

Of the vast library of books and materials Robin pours over in her studies of all things Disabilities, Jenny McCarthy is on her favorites list. You probably don't know who she is because you're a guy with a busy life and don't really keep track of celebrities. Well, then again, maybe you do because she's a hot Hollywood bombshell with all the assets of modern medicine.

She has a son with Autism and has been a good voice for the cause. She's written books about it, which my wife has read and I skim through. So when she went on Oprah, we sat down to watch. The one thing I remember is she told the viewers that her husband wasn't interested in helping their son. So she divorced him.

I thought that was odd because my neighbor, a single mother of a severely handicapped kid, said roughly the same thing, except that he chose to leave them. Turns out, it seems to be a common theme among single parents of kids with disabilities. Since that time, I have heard or read variations of the following on many occasions, "He didn't like having a handicapped child, so he left." "He couldn't handle our kid...our situation, so he abandoned us."

Stories of men abandoning their families for whatever reason are as plentiful as tourists on Waikiki Beach. These are sad stories and many are absolutely inexcusable, repulsive, and true. Let's face it. Our sex occupies better than 90% of the nations penitentiaries and as a whole, are a lot more stupid than our counter parts. I realize I am stating the obvious here, but If you need some reassurance or just want to take a break, go to youtube and type in "people doing stupid things" or anything like that, and enjoy the genius of the Y chromosome.

No man is exempt from the fallibility of manhood. Yet as unintelligent as we are, most of us have proven smart enough to avoid prison. And even though we have all done things that would be on

108

youtube's list of stupid things, we were smart enough not to have a camera running or at least destroyed the footage. Or if you're like me, you keep the evidence it in a safe place and bust it out when your friends need a side splitting laugh.

And still most of us manage to get by or excel in life, earn a living, convince a babe to marry us, and have a family. Incredible isn't it? As simpleminded as we are, we manage to do great things! And once we have established something remarkable like a family, we can still throw it all away.

When Jenny McCarthy went on Oprah and said her husband wasn't interested in helping their son so she divorced him, do you think that man is sitting home saying, yep, she's got that right?

I do not know Jenny McCarthy's ex husband or the thousands of divorced dads no longer with their families. They all have separate stories and reasons for leaving or being left behind. I am not sympathetic to the man who did not have the backbone to do everything in his power to keep his child from having a broken family. But to the man who exhausted all efforts, I do. Who really knows except that man? I don't know and you don't know except that their story has less to do with their child, disabled or not, and more to do with the relationship with their spouse.

Women love to talk while men love to not talk. It stands to reason that in breakups we are most likely to get the woman's story and not the man's. We want to dissect divorce so we can determine what went wrong. Human nature screams that one side was wrong. One side of the marriage was responsible for breaking the home. One side screwed up and now there is a child without a mother and father in the home.

It takes two to raise a child! It takes three or four to raise a child with special needs. But two is all you get! So you make do. Or maybe you do more and make that two so strong that they can do the work of three or four and reap the rewards of three or four.

It's difficult enough to be married. Add to it your special obstacles and challenges and the odds are certainly stacked against you. Good thing it's not all up to you. It's up to two!

Nobody Knows But YOU

Like a clown I put on a show the pain is real even if nobody knows and I'm crying inside and nobody knows it but me. "Nobody Knows" Kevin Rich

When you get up in the morning, you go through the morning ritual and out the door you go. When your wife gets up in the morning, she wants to look good. When she looks good, she feels good. She will spend the extra time in front of the mirror and in the closet picking out the day's ensemble.

You want to look good, sure, but it's nowhere near the degree that your wife wants. Look at your side of the closet and then look at hers. Who has more clothes and SHOES? Who has the newest outfits? If you happen to have new clothes it's because your wife wants you to look good and she got them for you. Same goes for her children. She wants them to look cute. Women buy a tremendous amount of clothes. They drive a multibillion dollar fashion industry. Why? Because they want others to think they look good, or their family looks good.

Who buys the gossip magazines? Who follows the latest trends? Who insists on family portraits and organizes the entire event including outfits? WOMEN DO! <u>Because public opinion matters to them more than it does to you.</u>

In many respects, the opinion of your wife's friends matters more than yours. Ever pick out furniture, paint colors, clothes, or anything with your wife? It is usually better if she goes and picks those things out with her besties. You may suggest the peach curtains over the cream shutters for the bathroom window. She might consider that, but probably not. But if her best friend suggests the same thing, it's more likely a fabulous idea.

I work with women who travel the world in search of the next biggest trends in fashion jewelry and apparel. I went to a trade show, a year ago, and asked three of these experts to help me get something for my wife. They perused hundreds of booths and assured me they had found the perfect gift.

The necklace was adorable, personal, inspirational, and selling like mad. Robin told me she liked the gift, though in the past year it has rarely been worn. This is a clear indicator that she really does not like it. If her sister had given her the necklace, or she saw the line of women I stood in to get it, that necklace would get at least 10 times more wear.

It's funny really, if you think about it. Robin and I have been married for 18 years. Pretty much from the beginning, she has made fun of my grubby, funny, and out-dated clothes. In turn, I make fun of her wearing the same jeans and outfits as everybody else. She cares, and I could care less. Yet these differences, though benign when we're talking about material things like clothes, is magnified to the 10th power when your kid is the subject.

This is a world of he said, she said. People on the outside looking in. It's not hard to find an arm chair quarterback standing on the sideline of your life who thinks they know best. It's human nature to stick our noses in other people's business. We scrutinize that boy for his history of bad behavior. Inside, you criticize his parents for lack of discipline. They must be horrible parents because that child lacks any kind of self-restraint. I'm sure there are no rules in that home.

Every now and then their son gets out and wanders aimlessly. Sometimes he'll bolt for the park or anywhere. Last time they lost him for an hour. Cops were called. The whole neighborhood was out looking for him. Honestly, they have got to do something different because obviously whatever they are doing isn't working.

That girl needs to cut her fingernails because she scratches others. That boy wears the same thing to school not two days in a row, but three! The kid over there has a P&J sandwich even though every parent knows there is a kid in class with a peanut allergy. That kid is a bully. This kid drools. That kid can't keep his hands to himself. This kid can't control his emotions. That kid pees his pants. This kid has a filthy mouth.

Children are not always a reflection of their parents. Sometimes there are problems, issues, handicaps, etc. Having a different kid can wreak havoc on families. People see kids and families on the outside and opinions are formed in seconds. You never really know what someone is dealing with on the inside, and yet how quick we are to judge.

You are tired of the way your kid acts in public and it's just too much work, so you begin to take rain checks on family outings. You stay at home more. Consequently your kid gets more time video gaming than you ever thought you would allow.

Have you altered your life because of what others think? Because that's wrong. Unless you agree with the arm chair quarterbacks, altering your life based on what people think, or what you or your wife think that other people think is a step in the wrong direction. Outside opinions are just that. And on the outside is where they belong for the most part.

There is one thing I know. And that is, nobody knows. Nobody knows but you! You live in your home. You and your wife are the head of the house and the ultimate authority on your children. I am not saying shut the world out and don't take advice or lessons from anywhere. I am saying, take all that in and cater it to your family. Leave out what needs to be left out, embrace truth, and alter that which needs to be altered. Because nobody knows the uniqueness of your wife and kids like you! Nobody knows but YOU!

When I say you, I mean the team of you and your wife. She will undoubtedly know the children and their needs best. Depending on your family dynamic, she most likely spends more time with them, takes care of them, and has better instincts in child rearing than you. But here is where things get interesting.

That kid with issues is your kid. You and your wife are trying to come together and address every embarrassing moment, each sensory overload, and outburst. Almost all the drama filled episodes are accompanied by opinions of others. You might be able to shake it on occasion. Who cares what others think. But for your wife, it's a whole other story.

Inevitably, the two of you make decisions to better your child's life. These decisions are based on information and feelings. Typically, I am more inclined to make decisions based on statistical information. For example: 80% of kids suffering from sleep apnea and/ or bedwetting are cured or show significant improvements when their adenoids are removed. Boom! Schedule the surgery! No more freaking out when he doesn't take a breath for an eternity and the stink has got to go!

Robin is more inclined to make decisions based on feelings. For example, she really likes our pediatrician's new office. It feels modern and clean and is well decorated. The staff is friendly and they greet her, so she feels comfortable with them. She likes the pediatrician well before she even sees him. At that point, the doc would really have to be sub-par for Robin not to like him or her. Because going from the front door to the reception desk is giving off nothing but good vibrations.

Robin and I coming together to solve problems is typical of many couples. I ask for factual information and Robin expresses her feelings. So you sort through the information and feelings and hopefully make the correct decisions. Note: between information and feelings, one of those methods is more likely to induce strong emotions (hint, it's not the gathering information method). So tread lightly when necessary or your meetings with your wife will be counterproductive, heated, and possibly entertaining for your neighbors.

Ideally, I'll be able to dig deep for my gut reaction and Robin will see value in all the facts and we will come to an agreeable conclusion. You might relate as these behaviors can be common in married couples.

But keep in mind what we have been talking about here! Your wife is more susceptible to public opinion than you are. You may at times need to reel her in a bit. I like to approach it like this. Honey, I really appreciate all the work you've done on this. I think I'm there with you. My only concern is that we might be favoring this diet, or class, or teacher, or thing, because the Jones had such success with it. Because, our kid is so different from theirs.

Your wife is also better tuned into your child's needs than you are. So reeling her in to what's best for your kid should come naturally. But, if you need to bring her in, I know you'll use your best Dale Carnegie husband skills. And let your wife know that just because the school psychologist, BFF, favorite IEP team member, or Fairy Godmother tells us Junior really needs summer school, he may benefit more by going camping with his family instead.

Nothing matters more than the people within the walls of your own home. The people you call family. That's what matters. And nobody knows them like you. NOBODY!

The Run Down

1. Be aware of public opinion and the arm chair quarterback and how it might influence you.

2. Your wife will be influenced more than you. May need to reel her in tactfully.

3. Nobody knows what goes on in your home, nor the people in it like you do. NOBODY!

Enough is Enough

Enough is enough is enough I can't go on, I can't go on, no more no

"No More Tears" Donna Summer

Robin's Tuesday Schedule

5:30 Wake, get dressed, go over plans for the day, fix breakfast

6:30 Wake Tyler and get him going. Read Tuesday morning social story with him. This is a story written about him, for him, and is designed to help him adjust better to the morning routine.

7:00 Wake other kids, get them dressed and eating breakfast

7:30 Out the door and drive to JR piano

7:45 Drop JR at piano and drive to Tyler's school

8:00 Play at school with Ty and make sure he gets to his class with minimal problems. Throughout the day, must monitor and be in communication with Ty's teacher and principal. Oftentimes he needs to be picked up early because his teacher and aides cannot handle him

8:30 Pick up JR from piano

8:40 Drop JJ off at preschool and haul butt to JR's school

9:00 Drop off JR at school (most of the time late).

9:15-11:30 Clean house, dishes, projects, ...

11:30 Drive to JJ's school

11:45 Pick up JJ

12:00-2:00 Run errands, groceries, etc.

2:30 Pick up Ty from school and conference with teachers, aides, principal

3:00 Pick up JR from school

3;00-3:30 Play at the park

4:00-4:30 Dr. appt. Robin takes Ty while Rick watches JR and JJ

5:00-6:00 Kaiser training program for the whole family

6:30-7:30 Homework

7:30-8:00 Bed routine, brush and floss teeth, Rick reads and tells stories.

8:00 Lights out

8:00-9:00 Deal with kids getting out of bed, catch up on email, phone calls, projects, research, plan, make kids lunches, lay out clothes for the next day.

9:00-10:00 Collapse on the couch in exhaustion and zone out of reality to your favorite show.

10:00 Lights out.

Many of you read that schedule and think, that's a full day. Some of you think that's normal. While others think, their day is busier. For us, most days are not this busy, but some days can be more busy. This means that I ditch work and try to make it up at night when everyone has gone to bed. Imagine living this routine or one similar to it day after day after day. As the years go by you may add to it extracurricular programs from sports to music to scouts to new doctors and universities who want to test, and all kinds of other Things.

Don't forget the dynamics of your family and possible fighting, whining, teasing, messes and fires to be contained or extinguished throughout the day. The stress of having a special needs child may require 100% of your time and effort every day. Putting out those fires can put us over the top. Was he sent home today? Did he hit or kick another kid, teacher, parent, or sibling? How can we get him to stop these behaviors? Why does he act like he does? Why is he different? How do we get him to change? When will he grow out of this phase? Will the next phase be worse? There is an infinitesimal amount of questions. And these things will drive even the most sane person over the edge.

Mama Bear does not know how to down shift. She runs hot all the time. Mama Bear feels like her special kid deserves the best. She is going to do everything in her power to make sure her kid has the best teachers, doctors, and Things not just for the cub, but for the whole family. And what about the siblings? Well, why should the other cubs be limited just because their sibling has a handicap? Don't worry, Mama Bear will run at full throttle to make sure every cub has what they need.

You can see it coming, can't you? The schedule is too demanding. Flames are crossing the fire line. Mama Bear has been running too hot for too long. A blowup is inevitable and there will be casualties. A growl comes in here, a snarl there, a couple snaps. Then Papa Bear leaves the toilet seat up and it's all over. "You're gonna' get your butt kicked!"

You Cannot Stop Mama Bear,

You Can Only Hope to Contain Her

In a way, each one of us has an El Guapo to face. For some, shyness might be their El Guapo. For others, a lack of education might be their El Guapo. For us, El Guapo is a big, dangerous man who wants to kill us. But as sure as my name is Lucky Day, the people of Santa Poco can conquer their own personal El Guapo, who also happens to be *the actual* El Guapo! Lucky Day, The Three Amigos

Is living a daily demanding schedule with work, kids, friends, Things, special diets, etc. worth a child losing a parent in his home? The answer of course is positively NO! But it happens. And it happens a lot!

Are you willing to trust peer or outside influences more than your own feelings and convictions as Patriarch of your home? Because that's not right!

What statistic will you contribute to? Will you continuously work to build a stronger marriage and solidify the foundation of your family? Or will you throw in the towel?

Can you take a Mama Bear butt kicking? Can you take the licks and do so for no other reason than you are Papa Bear? You are an easy target and Mama Bear has been pushed over the edge. Can you take the heat, and do so time and time again, without throwing it back in her face? Can you? If so, for how long? Because you love Mama Bear. You need Mama Bear. The maternal instinct to nurture and protect is essential to your family.

Depending on the nature of your wife and the degree to which Mama Bear rears up, you may be taking your lumps occasionally, or all the freaken' time! Fight the urge to argue. If your sweet wife says the sky is purple, you can suggest that it may appear that way, but it's really quite blue. But if Mama Bear say's the sky is purple, than by golly, how did the sky get so purple! You get the difference? I'm sure you do.

118

Plenty of couples have split up over far less than what you will face in your situation. Can you decipher between your wife and Mama Bear? Because you don't treat them the same. Timing and tact play vital rolls in your marriage and you are about to become an expert. You have to be. The success of your life and family depend on it.

After years of studying all kinds of parents with every kind of challenge, I like to entertain the question: Are kids with special needs born to awesome parents? Or do weak or average parents become awesome because of their kid with special needs?

The answer is.... YES!

In order to be that awesome Dad, you need to overcome the obstacles of having a different child. And that involves caring for your wife more than it does caring for your child. Some might think that doesn't sound right. But you think about what is best for your kid. The very best thing you could ever give him. That one thing which will give her or him the best chance for success and development and happiness, is the blessing of a loving mother and father in the home. That, my friend, is what it's all about.

So when Mama Bear sends you running to your cave, think of this. You love Mama Bear. You don't want to stop her. You need a woman who will fight for your child and stand up for your family. There are so many kids neglected and kicked to the curb because of passive parents. Many kids, especially those with special needs are at a disadvantage because their mom lets the system take over and blindly trusts her child's placement and circumstance. But not your kid! No! Mama Bear is taking care of your kid.

Her fuse may be short. Her patience absent. Her temper at a boil. Her common sense cut short. These are simply short lived by-products of Mama Bear. And you need Mama Bear. So instead of sulking in the doghouse because your woman has taken her frustrations out on you, count your blessings, because your kid has a Bear looking out for him!

Although there are times when you need to get out of her way, Mama Bear can be contained. It won't be easy, but you simply need to keep it together man, and come up with real solutions. Here are a few suggestions...

Part III
Happy Wife Happy Life

It Just Doesn't Matter

And even if we win, if we win, HAH! Even if we win! Even if we play so far above our heads that our noses bleed for a week to ten days; even if God in Heaven above comes down and points his hand at our side of the field; even if every man woman and child held hands together and prayed for us to win, it just wouldn't matter because all the really good looking girls would still go out with the guys from Mohawk because they've got all the money! It just doesn't matter if we win or we lose. IT JUST DOESN'T MATTER!

Bill Murray, Meatballs

Robin and I started our family in Key West, Florida. Everything we did there revolved around the water. Where we worked, played, and lived all had to do with the ocean and we loved it. Our landlord and best friend was a lesbian. We spent countless hours on the water with her. Funny thing about being in the Keys and especially out on the water, there seems to be no boundaries or etiquette about topics of discussion. Filter-less conversation can really make you think and split your side at the same time.

She was a month into a new relationship when we were out on her boat lobster diving. As the evening approached and we were staring at a cooler full of lobster, we took a moment to relax on the boat and let the free game conversation flow. Believe me, you'd love to be a fly on the wall with one conservative heterosexual couple and one liberal gay couple on a small boat miles out at sea.

The gay couple had just had their first major spat. It was apparent from our conversation that the spat was lingering on. They peppered Robin and me about our arguments and how we resolved them, but they were not satisfied with our answers. I finally said, "Look, I have not won a single argument and don't intend to. Robin wins every time. Because we know Robin wins and I lose, there isn't anything to fight about. I have yet to find something that I am so passionate about that I'd want to fight my wife over it."

Still not satisfied, the new girl, with emotion in her voice asks me, "but what if you are right?!" To which I replied, "It doesn't matter who is right and who is wrong. Do you want to be right? Or do you want to be happy?" She then yelled out in serious jest, "I want to be right!" This brought a roar of laughter from everyone.

I actually continued this conversation later with our landlady/BFF. Again, this is all serious, but in good humor. There were few secrets between us. I told her I didn't know many lesbian couples, so I didn't understand how they did it. I said, "One of you has got to take the role of the guy, right? Someone has to be wrong. Someone has to take the blame for anything that goes wrong. And someone has to say sorry. If you don't have that, how can you have a happy relationship?"

One of the great things about being a guy is that most stuff just doesn't matter. So it is easier to be wrong, or take the blame, or say sorry. If your wife wants to eat at Olive Garden and not TGI Fridays, that's cool. If she wants to paint a bedroom blue instead of green, you're good with that. Even if it's an ugly blue that doesn't go with anything, you are not going to lose sleep over it. We will go along with what she wants to do because it just doesn't matter to us. Who cares about all the trivial decisions? What does it really matter?

Think about all the choices you make every day. Think about the last argument you had with your wife. What was it about? Chances are almost for sure that it is not that big of a deal for you and certainly not worth a fight. Very few things really matter. They may matter to Mama Bear, but not to you. That is the beauty of being a guy.

Personally, my wife, in her current state, is less opinionated than most women. She prefers for me to make a lot of decisions or at least help her. If you haven't been able to tell, I do have a lot of opinions. But if she feels strongly about more vegetables in our diet and then busts out the Haagen-Dazs after the kids have gone to bed, shoot, I'm in. Why does it even matter?

"Type A"

The following conversation was between myself and our good friend, Virginia. We were sitting in lawn chairs watching our boys play little league baseball.

Virginia: I talked to your mom at the last game. That was nice of her to take Jefferson to the game.

Rick: Yes, she's great to have around.

Virginia: I had an interesting conversation with her. We were talking about how well you and Robin get along. I mentioned that the two of you were a good fit with Robin and her type A personality and you with your type B personality.

Rick: (Laughing)

Virginia: Do you know what your mom said? She said that you were a classic type A personality. I couldn't believe it. She rattled off all these character traits that I have never seen in you.

Rick: Look, I have always been type A. I'm that guy who lives by a schedule, to do lists, take charge and get it done. However, Robin is also a Type A. Two type A's living together, locking horns and raising these kids was too difficult. It was too stressful and not working out, so I switched to type B.

Virginia: (slight jaw drop, puzzled look)

Rick: I'm a convert type B. So yes, you are right, I am more of a type B personality. My mother hasn't been around much in the last year to notice the change. She raised me. So, to her, I'll always be that high energy in your face get the task done at all costs kid.

Change

"I guess what I'm trying to say, is that if I can change, and you can change, everybody can change!" Rocky Balboa (Rocky IV)

For the record, I think the Rocky line referenced here is the worst of all the Rocky motivational speeches. However, it's my Dad's favorite, and he has helped me a little on this book, so I'm throwing it in for him. Plus the only other thing I can think of at the moment for this section is the Brady Bunch singing "Time to Change."

We have already covered how women undergo personality changes. These changes can occur without notice or reason. However, the main change we have covered is the metamorphosis into Mama Bear. This change happens for a specific reason. You should know it is coming.

Men on the other hand gloat in the fact that we never change. Hopefully there is some maturing during the early years and growth throughout your life. But for the most part, we are basically the same guy from here to there. Subtle to radical change can and does occur however. Sometimes it is a bad change. But hopefully it is good.

I would love to say that making the change from a type A personality to a type B was not a big deal. Truth is it was hard for me, especially when I knew my way was more efficient or made more sense. But when Mama Bear is running around with the pedal to the metal in high gear, beware that even the most benign or well-intended comment can be interpreted as a threat.

Let me make a few suggestions on good change. Heed these words when Mama Bear is out. We could write books on this, but for now, we'll keep it brief.

1. Ease up on the reins big fella! Now is not the time to assert your place of dominance at the head of the house. Grasping

125

for any power now is a horrible idea. Many of you can't help it and do this involuntarily. That's because you are insecure. Let it go. Let it go (Apollo's trainer voice, Rocky II).

2. Learn to use little to NO words. Now is not the time to show off your genius by telling your wife that with gas at $4 a galleon, and her time at a premium, she is much better off buying online instead of randomly driving all over the country in search of that perfect gift. She does not need your input on how she's doing. Fight that urge to tell her that gift will be returned anyway and doesn't need to be perfectly wrapped. SHUT-JO-MOUF!

3. Slow the game down. When emotions are high is when we make the worst mistakes. Play within yourself. Don't get caught up in the heat of any moment. Relax and be slow to react. If this is met with resistance, remember, it is better to be accused of slow or no reaction than it is to react wrongly.

4. Roll with the punches. A verbal jab here from a guy at work, an uppercut remark from a family member, and even a bad report kick to the crotch from your kid. Blows are going to come. They will come in all sorts of ways. How you take the blow is entirely up to you. If you take it head on and get knocked back by absorbing the full force, you will eventually get knocked out. However, if you glance to the side and lessen the blow with a roll, you'll be ready for the next punch, and the next, and the next.

5. Be not easily offended. This is closely related with number 4. You cannot afford to get caught up in the offended games. It will eat you up! An offender reacts in accordance with what they know and what their experiences are. Chances are great that the offense has more to do with the person dishing it out than the one it is intended for. Don't give it the time of day. It isn't worth it.

Mean People Suck

I'm starting with the man in the mirror

Michael Jackson

Every now and then I am reminded that there are guys out there who just suck. There's the angry guy with the chip on his shoulder. The guy who wants to rip you off. The road rage guy. The drunk guy at the ball park dropping the F-bomb every sentence. The tough guy, the snob, the hothead. Have I got to you yet?

If you read through this chapter and think to yourself, whoa, I'm not going to be subservient to my wife. I am the head of the house. I make the decisions around here. I am not going to let my wife dictate everything. She's got to respect me and my decisions.

If you have a special needs child, and you have that machismo attitude, you haven't got a chance. You were born in the wrong century. Your chances of having a successful marriage were slim to begin with. Add a special needs child and you can forget it. The only chance you have is if you married a woman from a culture that tolerates male chauvinism.

If you are even leaning that way, you've got to let that go. Do you want to keep it together man? Then you have got to let that attitude go. For the sake of your family, you've got to chill and lose the ego. Vanity, arrogance, and pride are a one-way ticket to visitation on weekends. Do you really want your special kid without a father? Think about it.

Are you so self-absorbed and insecure that you need to puff out your chest to let everyone know you're the man? Because all that does is let everyone know you are a thug with no self respect.

Swallow your pride and embrace real manhood, where we keep our emotions in check and are offended by nothing. Where we have enough self-worth to roll with the punches instead of punching back. Where we are confident enough to slow the game down and keep silent or our words in check. We love our wives. We don't fight with them. We might fight with our brothers, but when we do it's over and forgotten faster than it began.

The Closer

During the more than 15 years Trevor Hoffman played for the San Diego Padres, they were not very good. They went to the World Series in 1998 and made it interesting a couple more of those years, but mostly, they just were not very good. There were a few silver linings of those teams, and one of them was all-star closer, Trevor Hoffman.

Few people outside of San Diego can really appreciate Trevor Hoffman because they did not get to see him that much. The Padres were not good, so a nationally televised game was rare. You only got to see him whenever he played in your market. And when the Padres had the lead heading into the last inning. Trevor was really famous for two things. An unbelievable change-up and his ability to forget.

Giving up a run or blowing a save didn't happen too often. But when it did, judging by the way he played, he could not remember it. It was like it never happened. Give up a homer over the wall in left-center? Next batter, comes to the plate and he can't seem to remember he just gave up a bomb. Boom, three pitches later, the batter unscrews himself out of the batters box and heads dejected into the dugout. Blow a save? The next day rolls around and Trevor doesn't have the slightest idea what happened the game before. It's three up, three down, game over.

Women have long complained about men and their deficient memories. What I can't figure out is why women don't celebrate it? Look, guys, pay attention here... Get the big dates locked in, anniversary, birthdays, couple events that are important to your wife. Of course all the great memories you have created with your family is all easy stuff. But the bad events, well, those can all go.

Our ability to forget is truly awesome! Does your wife want you remembering every time she screwed up? Every time she said something hurtful and full of venom? Her bad days? Her fat days? Her lazy days? Her mistakes? What would be the purpose?

We are the closers for our team. We come in at the bottom of the 9th to save the game. Our selective memory takes in the good and bad, learns from it, than discards the trash. Why hang onto garbage? It will only weigh us down and make us stink. Forgive, forget and move on.

The Run Down

1. Most things just don't matter to us.

2. Change for the good.

    A. Ease up on the reins

    B. Learn to use little to NO words

    C. Slow the game down

    D. Roll with the punches

    E. Be not easily offended

3. Mean People Suck.

    A. Lose the caveman attitude

    B. Embrace real manhood

4. You are the closer.

    A. Take it all in, remember the good, release the garbage

Antecedent

Dark Helmet: What the hell am I looking at? When does this happen in the movie?

Colonel Sandurz: Now. You're looking at now, sir. Everything that happens now, is happening now.

Dark Helmet: What happened to then?

Colonel Sandurz: We passed then.

Dark Helmet: When?

Colonel Sandurz: Just now. We're at now, now.

Dark Helmet: Go back to then.

Colonel Sandurz: When?

Dark Helmet: Now.

Colonel Sandurz: Now?

Dark Helmet: Now.

Colonel Sandurz: I can't.

Dark Helmet: Why?

Colonel Sandurz: We missed it.

Dark Helmet: When?

Colonel Sandurz: Just now.
Space Balls

One of the many Things we attended was a Children's Hospital program that lasted a few months. There was a lot of homework and training. We would meet with a specialist and watch Tyler through a two-way mirror playing in another room. We would analyze everything. What his movements were, his behaviors, and why he did what he did. One of the topics we went over until I was sick, was the antecedent.

The antecedent is the thing or event that happened before the behavior or event. Basically, whatever preceded or took place before. For example, Tyler would have a total melt-down after going into a noisy room. Because he heard loud noises (antecedent) he would have a melt-down. If the teacher announces it's reading time, Tyler will run out of the class. If he drinks water before going to bed, he will pee the bed. Announcing reading time and drinking water are the antecedents.

Man oh man, we had antecedent discussions, roll play, homework, you name it. You can change behaviors and just about everything if you know what the antecedent is. If you know what it is, then you can change it, thus changing the behavior or outcome. If Tyler goes to a ball game, we put these airline noise canceling headphones over his ears. His teacher now finds creative ways to get into reading time, and we watch him like a hawk to make sure he doesn't drink before bed. We have changed the antecedents and therefore changed the outcome.

The Thing was to learn about antecedents for Tyler, but I learned a more valuable lesson. I have antecedents, you have them, and most importantly, *your wife has them.*

What Men Know About Women

Cricket chirp

I went to a seminar once and the speaker talked about this book called, "What Men Know About Women." It has this great cover and you open it up to find that it's filled with nothing but blank pages. It's a great gag gift and got plenty of laughs. And speaking of laughs, is there an end to, 'men know nothing about women humor?' Seems like it's as old as time.

I wonder if Eve got together with her daughters and bagged on Adam, "Seriously, you guys have no idea. Adam snores like a bear in labor, so you think I get any sleep! Then I'm like, thank goodness he's up early and I can finally close my eyes. Seriously, five minutes later he decides it's time to castrate a sheep! Don't you think he knows I would like to sleep! You know he still wears the same fig leaf from the Garden of Eden? It's disgusting! I can't get him to throw anything away. You know what I mean? Ugh, it's sooooo frustrating because he never listens to me and forgets everything!"

What Eve doesn't realize is that Adam remembers almost everything. He simply chooses to forget. Sometimes ignorance is bliss. For many of you, ignorance is bliss all the time. Adam listens to Eve every time she speaks, even when the talking turns into nagging. But because Adam doesn't agree or do exactly what Eve tells him to do, Eve accuses him of not listening.

The truth is, husbands know their wives far better than anyone will admit. We simply don't want to blow our cover. The more man knows, the more he is accountable when something goes wrong. Better to play ignorant sometimes. Plus it's funny, so we keep it alive. But in most cases the notion that men know nothing about their wives simply is not true.

Chances are you know your wife better than anyone. You probably know her better than she knows herself. You know what makes her happy. You know what makes her sad. You know her favorite things and what she finds annoying, offensive, and adorable. You live with her 24/7. And although the female is a complex maze of plots and personalities, you've gone down that road countless times. Remember, nobody knows her but you. Think about it for awhile.

How accurate can you be on all things pertaining to your wife? Everything from food preferences to movies? What about mood swings, friends, reactions to situations like emergencies, weather, academics, current events, goals, dislikes, and her dreams. You know when she's on her period or about to be. Many of you have it on an internal calendar of your own, or a calendar your wife doesn't see.

Admit it! Nobody's perfect of course, but you can accurately predict her actions, her needs, her thoughts, her wants. You don't sit around and think about it and try to predict things, because that's not what we do. Nor do we want to. For sure you are far more accurate than she will ever admit. So give yourself credit and have confidence. You know your wife. If you don't, pay attention, because life is about to get a little sweeter.

Antecedents in Action

"Sis Boom Bah" the answer to the question, "What sound do you hear when a sheep explodes? "... Johnny Carson as Carnac the Magnificent, The Tonight Show

Like *Punxsutawney Phil,* you have the ability to see into the future. And because you can do that, you can alter the outcome. My kids are very difficult to get them to bed if I let them watch TV until 8:30PM. I change the antecedent, and turn all electronics off at 7:30. Everyone gets to bed earlier and everyone is better behaved and better off.

Your wife is spent and yelling at the end of the day. She is upset at several things including a messy house. You pick one chore that you know she hates the most, usually the dishes, and get it done. Wife is appreciative and in a better mood.

Previously, we have discussed getting out in front of situations. For example, the best teacher, who is perfect for your kid, teaches at the worst school in the district. Nobody wants to send little Emma to this school especially your wife, who is worried what her friends might think. But Emma is going to that school. Because, as we discussed in that chapter, *It's All About the Teacher.* You already had that discussion with your wife and both of you agreed that it's all about the teacher!

133

In the chapter, _Nobody Knows But You_, you and your bride got together as a team before any more decisions were made. You both decided you would not be influenced by what friends thought. This is right along those lines. It's amazing what you can do when you get out in front of things. You know the antecedents! They may not always be simple and experimentation is essential, because it does not work every time, and sometimes you try something that works better. But you can change the antecedents to make life a little sweeter. For example...

Know When to Say When

You've got to know when to hold 'em
Know when to fold 'em
Know when to walk away
And know when to run

Kenny Rogers The Gambler

In the Chapter, "Enough is Enough," we discussed the rigors of your wife's daily schedule. This is a schedule she is unwilling to compromise because Mama Bear demands the best for her cubs. The mere notion that the family schedule should change, for any reason, puts her on the defensive. Despite your best intentions, you end up in the doghouse where you hang another portrait.

CHANGE THE ANTICEDENT! You have got to get out in front of this before it gets to that point. For those of you in the beginning stages, perhaps you are coming out of denial and you realize your kid has issues. Here is a suggestion. And I am urging you, NAY, PLEADING WITH YOU! You must do this! No matter if you just found out or you're in the trenches. You need to get this done!

Don't fall for the complacency you might be in. Maybe you are so satisfied with your life and marriage and your wife is just so supportive and wonderful. You had a heart to heart and you have never been more in love than you are now. You are this inseparable team of power, unafraid of anything! Even when you fart, it smells like roses.

You are ready to take on the world and see no need to do what I am about to tell you. BUT YOU MUST! Because as good as things are now, you don't have a clue what will happen next week, next month, or next year! And when things are good, that is the best time to do this! Also, there is not a downside! There is no reason not to do this. Don't get complacent. Get 'er done.

TIMING IS EVERYTHING. You have got to get your wife in an agreeable mood. For some of you, that's all the time. And for some of you, that is none of the time or something in-between. Remember, you know your wife. If you need to take her out, bring her chocolates, plan something fun, YOU DO IT! Because this is *very important, muy importante!* Get it? Got it? Good!

WARNING: Attempting this without prior knowledge that your wife is in a fabulous mood could cause pain, suffering, and extended visits in the doghouse.

After you have properly prepped the subject, or she is naturally there, you may proceed with your mission.

Objective: You and your wife must agree or commit to the following.

1. **A happy marriage and home is the most important thing we can do for our children.** This is the basis of this book! There are no exceptions to this rule. Family experiences and relationships are uniquely special. Nothing can act as a substitute for love at home. This should be an easy topic. Talk about your wedding and experiences together. The growth from the trials and rewards of life together. Talk about happy events. The two of you started this together and have built a foundation. Take your time on this and make sure everyone's priorities are in order.

2. **We have a different family. The road to success with our special kid will be filled with ups and downs, successes and defeats, but we are a team and will take it on together.** Since you are new to this, fear and uncertainty are normal. That's a downer. But no worries! There will be more ups than a rocket heading to the stars. Different family means different sacrifices and way of living. Not inferior, just divergent.

135

3. **I am your coach and you are mine.** Before we walk out of the house, my gorgeous wife asks me how she looks. My answer is almost always in the affirmative. But occasionally I can find a piece of food in her hair from feeding Eli or a run in her stocking where another kid thought she would bite. She in turn looks at me and tells me my pants have stains on them and my shoulders are crusty from too much dried snot.

   I can see things on her she cannot see for herself, and vice versa. Don't be surprised if your wife knows you better than you know yourself. You're an easy creature to understand. Accept the fact that she can see if you are traveling down the wrong road. Maybe you are burning the candle at both ends and she can see you are getting ugly and not prioritizing correctly. She should not hesitate to ask you to scale down, get an exercise program, or whatever she thinks you need. You should be able to do the same.

4. **Know when to say when.** And by that I mean, know when to eliminate Things, routines, or people that make it tougher on your family. Families with special needs often times need to simplify. If your family is constantly running then you are living in the red zone. That is not where you want to be. If you run in the red zone for too long, then you will crash and burn. This is a difficult subject and vital to #1 above. Know when to say when. Got a regular Thing in your life that is no longer worth your time and effort? Say good-bye. Have a friend or family member who is zapping the energy out of you? Make changes. Your spouse and kids are more important. Do not flirt with living in the red zone. I like the rule that either one in the marriage can call a timeout at any time and discuss the situation. You need to establish a pact that you eliminate Things or events or dial them back when life starts to stretch you too thin. Passing the break-

ing point of living in the red zone is in direct violation of rule number one and can be detrimental to everyone living under your roof.

I hope that conversation was meaningful and enjoyable for both of you. Meetings like these can really give you both a shot in the arm. Empowering your spouse are exceptional moments. Try to end this conversation like you would a notable event. Because that is exactly what it was. The more memorable you can make this conversation, the better. Make it special, maybe at a distinct location or part of an occasion.

Now don't get cocky! You are not out of the woods yet. There are three important steps you must follow if and when you ever need to call your spouse on this agreement. They are:

1. Follow up

2. Follow up

3. Follow up

That memorable empowering conversation and everything that went into it, is all for not, unless you follow up. In the weeks, months, and years to follow, you must on occasion bring up this pact the two of you have made. Always make it positive and appreciative. One easy way of doing it is to ask your wife how you are doing. "Hey honey, remember when we made that agreement that we would watch out for each other? I feel like I've been struggling a bit lately. How am I doing?" You are a lucky man if she calls you out and has suggestions for you first.

For obvious reasons, never use that approach I just suggested if there is something you want to call her on. And speaking of calling her out, just because you made the pact doesn't mean you have to use it. It may never be necessary. But if you do need to use it, don't be weak or militant. This is a safety net, not a trump card. If Mama Bear is out and making wrong choices, you have got to wait or create a more conducive environment.

Can you make her laugh? A good belly laugh can cure just about anything for at least a time. Play it real smooth. Be sweet, kind, and use every bit of compassion you can muster. Remember, timing is everything and this should never be part of an argument. The more emotional you get the worse your decision process. Resist the temptation to bring up the agreement if things get heated.

The Run Down

1. Antecedent

    A. The thing or event that happened before the behavior or event

2. What Men Know About Women

    A. Contrary to popular belief, men do know about women

3. Antecedents in Action

    A. Find out what the antecedent is

    B. You have the power to change everything

    C. Get out in front of it

4. Know When To Say 'When'

    A. Change the antecedent

        1. Agree to the following:

            a. A happy marriage and home is *the most important* thing we can do for our child(ren).

            b. We have a different family

            c. I am your coach and you are mine

            d. Know when to say 'when'

    B. Follow up

    C. Be sweet. Don't be weak

Communication Breakdown

Communication breakdown, it's always the same. Havin' a nervous breakdown, drive me insane, ow, suck...

Communication Breakdown: Led Zeppelin

You line up at wide receiver. Your wife is under center. She moves her hand to her hip thus signaling you to run a quick slant. The play begins and you run a post because you did not see the signal. Quarterback throws the quick slant where you should be and it is intercepted. The players go to the sidelines and your wife asks why you didn't run the quick slant? You reply that you didn't see the signal. She huffs, rolls her eyes and walks away. This was your fault.

Next series you break from the huddle and spot yourself on the line in the wide-out position. You focus on the quarterback. If she audibles out of the called play, you are ready. Sure enough she looks at you and puts her hand on her hip. You know what to do. But wait! She is also tapping her foot, which is the sign for a ten yard out. The play is about start and you are not sure what signal to go with. Quickly, you notice the opposition is showing the exact same defense the last time your wife gave you the signal for the quick slant. You are confident, and half a second later, run the slant. Your wife sees that you have run the wrong pattern again and is forced to throw the ball out of bounds. You apologize. Your fault.

When you get back to the huddle the QB is upset.

QB: Why didn't you run the out?

WR: I noticed both signals. The hip signal was given first and you did not wave it off before the foot tap signal. Also, the defense was running the same play they did before when you wanted me to do the slant. So I ran the slant.

QB: I NEVER PUT MY HAND ON MY HIP! UGH!

To say anything more would be a detriment to yourself and your team. You stay silent. Your bad.

Because of the conversation, she is late getting the play called. Your position is 20 yards farther away than anyone else and you get called for illegal procedure because you were not set when the center hiked the ball. You apologize to the team. Again, your bad.

The next play you run an in-route across the center of the field. Quarterback airmails it five feet over your head. You go up for it anyway, because that's the kind of player you are! Also, you want your QB to see you are working hard and willing to take risks. On the way down the strong safety hits you in the gut thus folding your body like a lawn chair and you end up gasping for breath as you lay on the turf.

Your quarterback comes over to check on you. She looks at you struggling for breath. She asks if you are okay and tells you to calm down and take slow breaths. You slowly get up with the aid of the trainer and your quarterback says, "Hey, if you are going to take the hit anyway, you might as well make the catch." Clearly your fault.

The next play is third and long. A beautiful pass is completed to the second string wide receiver who came in while you suck wind on the sidelines. He makes a good play and gets the first down. He makes another play and the offense is starting to click. Everyone is happy including you, because you are a team guy. But you get the feeling the quarterback prefers the second stringer.

A few plays go by and you start to get a little more air in your lungs. Still sucking air, you notice your ribs are really hurting especially when you move. So you check them to see if they might be broke. The next play is another pass to the second stringer. The ball hits him in the chest and bounces directly into the hands of the linebacker. That turnover would have never happened had you been in the game. Sooo, your fault!

Still not breathing correctly and feeling the pain of your rib injury, you suck it up and get back on field for the next series. The quarterback is fuming now. She does not talk to you. She does not look or even glance in your direction. This game thus far has been a disaster, and it is all entirely your fault.

The next series begins with two running plays that don't amount to much. It seems like she is trying to stay away from you. She calls the third down play in the huddle and the defense is set up perfectly for the play. But the QB thinks she is smarter than the Offensive Coordinator and changes the play. She stares you down and puts her hand on her hip and taps her foot. Luckily, you have had time to think about the last time she gave you both of those signals. You think the hand on the hip thing accentuated the foot tapping. Or in other words, what the quarterback was saying was, you had better run a darn good ten yard out and catch the freaken ball.

You are ready to make the play happen except she adds an unmistakable stink eye to the equation! Giving you the stink eye means to run a deep fade. In less than a second you surmise that putting her hand on her hip, which is now sticking out, and her foot tapping, which is moving so forcefully, it is wearing a divot into the turf, are both exclamation points to the third signal.

The center snaps the ball and you take off on a fade route. It was the perfect call. You have easily beaten the defensive back. The ball is a tight spiral to the optimal location just like you have practiced it a hundred times before. There is no one between you and the goal line as the ball descends to your waiting hands. You have guessed right! You knew what she was thinking! And now you will be the hero!

Except that ball goes right through your hands and hits the ground incomplete. Your diving sprawl to the turf following the incompletion will surely make ESPN's Not Top Ten Plays. Despite your best efforts, this is your worst blunder. The QB most likely thinks you missed the ball intentionally to get back at her for something?

To make matters worse, the incident occurred on the opposite sidelines from where your team is. The jog to the bench across the entire field with your tail between your legs seemed like a mile. You position yourself as far away from your teammates as possible and keep your head on a swivel ever watchful for your quarterback, who is fuming. You know it is coming. You can hear her voice in your head saying, you never get the signs! You never listen! You always drop the ball! You've heard it all before and it doesn't get easier.

You would rather skip the confrontation and go straight to the doghouse, but you know beat down is coming. All of a sudden a figure stands over you. You look up and it's Coach Kinsfather. He looks at you and says, "Boy, I ain't gonna' lie to you. You are going to get your butt kicked."

Language Lessons

I cannot say 'Language Lessons' without thinking of the 1980's classic movie, *Better Off Dead*. In that movie, language lessons referred to the international language of love. For you and me it applies to avoiding arguments. That's all. Most couples communicate just fine until someone is offended. Guess who that usually is? And so we learn her language like no one else, because fighting accomplishes nothing, is not productive, and often cannot be taken back. So you avoid going down that road at all costs. Here are a couple pearls to hold on to, some discussed previously and some not.

Technology is your friend, not a substitute. Text messaging was invented by a man. What a tremendous asset that is for us. You and your wife send clear, short messages to each other. It does not disrupt your day, you can answer it when you want, and directions are logged into your phone so you can flash back to it. Do not discount emails, other messaging services, and sharing the same calendar, as they are huge as well. Use technology often to make sure you and your wife are on the same page. Also use it to let your wife know you are thinking about her. Warning! Technology does not take the place of actual face-to-face conversations.

Keep it in perspective. Honey, this game will be over in 10 minutes is exactly proportional to your wife telling you she will be ready in

142

10 minutes. You are different people belonging to different sexes. Keep it in perspective, and you'll keep it together, man.

Do not avoid face-to-face conversations. Often conversations between you and the Mrs. do not interest you. You do not feel the need to talk about feelings because you're cool. The problems she sees are not problems to you. You feel like it is unproductive and a waste of time. She asks your opinion on something. But you know your opinion does not matter because she is going to do what she wants. And you are fine with that, because you are a guy and it just doesn't matter to you. Your mind is searching for what she wants to hear because the time and energy it takes from you is too much. My friends... dig deep, focus on her, listen and participate. Do this often enough that you get good at it. Getting bad at it leads to a build up then a tussle and then the dark side.

"A man convinced against his will is of the same opinion still" Dale Carnegie. It is just as true for women and even more true for Mama Bear. Trying to convince your wife that she is wrong is a no win situation. Any spat from trying that is definitely your fault.

Endure. In the football example above, was there anything you could change to avoid the outcome? Not really. It's just what happens. It is your fault. Say you are sorry and endure. There is no fighting with Mama Bear. The only problem is when you say you are sorry too many times or say only what your wife wants to hear. And then she calls you on it. "You are not sorry; you just want to get out of this mess." She is right and both of you know it. In the entire universe, there is no known solution to this problem. Endure and hold your tongue.

Hold your tongue. Silence is golden some of the time. Know when that time is. Remember, you know your wife better than anyone. Two of our sons have too many therapy appointments that require too many hours, energy, and driving. My wife knows I feel this way. There is no need to bring it up again, so I don't. Mama Bear is going to do what she wants.

Timing is everything. Seems like I've heard this before? You know her moods, what she likes and dislikes and when. True, I prefer discussing potential problems in the morning or at least as far away from nighttime as possible. I prefer hashing out big issues when my wife is in a good mood. I prefer dissecting our children's needs on a POG. Why? Because timing is everything and this can make all the difference.

Avoid third party. If you need counseling, fine. But do not ever bring a third party friend into your relationship in hopes of validating your frustrations. Your marriage is your marriage. Her problem is your problem. Work it out… Come on man!

Antecedent. If you can get out in front of potential issues, you are the man! If you can schedule times and places and rules within your marriage and family, you've gone to Jedi level.

"I believe in science" Esqueleto, Nacho Libre. Yeah, you need to avoid this too. Although this is okay for women, it is not for you. I actually know a guy who gave an article like this to his wife after she got upset with him. "If your husband tunes you out when you quarrel (discuss?), don't blame him, blame his wiring. New research suggests that when men are tense, the part of their brains that reads facial expressions and emotions shuts down, which make them withdraw."[5] As you can imagine, Mama Bear doesn't give a rip that your wiring makes you forget her birthday or be less emotional. There are dozens of articles out there that will say exactly what you want to hear. Even if it is all true, suck it up and keep it together man!

"I want a new drug" Huey Lewis and the News. I grew up not far from the neighborhood haircutting lady. Most of my friends plus their siblings and moms went to this lady. I got my haircuts from her too. When I was 12, I sat in the haircutting chair and started asking questions about all the products on her shelves. Long story short, the conversation metamorphosed into every mom I knew dyed her hair. What! What about David's mom? What about Mike's mom? What about Ryan's mom? You're telling me they all have grey hair and so they all dye their hair? You have got to be kidding me! I was stunned.

Twenty years later I had the exact same experience finding out how many moms took drugs. Whoa! I was stunned again. I could not believe how many women needed some kind of anti depressant, anti anxiety, a stimulant, a downer, or something to help them cope and get through the day. The numbers are growing as more women are popping and more drug makers are filling needs.

Medicating Mama Bear is not as simple as getting a dart gun and hunkering down behind a blind. Although there will be plenty of times when you will want to do just that. It needs to come from her and discussed thoughtfully and thoroughly and not when you are tired. DO NOT MAKE DECISIONS WHEN YOU ARE TIRED OR EMOTIONS RUN HIGH. Also, use the same rule we discussed for medicating kids. Medicating Mama Bear should be after all other options are exhausted.

The Rundown

1. Whose Fault is it? It's your fault! Every time!

2. Language Lessons. Learn your wife's language

    A.   Technology is your friend, not a substitute

    B.   Keep it in perspective

    C.   Do not avoid face-to-face conversations

    D.   A man convinced against his will is of the same opinion still.

    E.   Endure

    F.   Hold your tongue

    G.   Timing is everything

    H.   Avoid third party

    I.   Antecedent

    J.   I believe in Science

    K.   I want a new drug

Who is Number One

"Look out for number one and try not to step in number two."

Rodney Dangerfield

Who is the most important person in your life? Who is number one? Who do you care for the most? Who do you think about the most, cherish the most, love the most, serve the most? This is not a rhetorical question. There is an actual answer so take time to think about it, because it is essential to your life.

Who is number one in your life? Who takes first priority? Who gets your time, your energy, your talents? Is it your boss or your work? Is it your video games? Internet gambling? Basketball team? Or could it be your kid(s)? Certainly we have talked a lot about kids, but even more than kids, we have talked about your wife. How to communicate. How to deal with her. How she might change. Is she the most important person in your life? Probably. But that my friend is not correct. The number one person in your life should undoubtedly be you. YOU ARE NUMBER ONE!

This is not a selfish thing. This is not about boosting your ego as lord over your castle. On the contrary, you take care of you because your castle needs it. Your castle and everyone therein benefits from a healthy positive leader. You must take care of you so you can be that leader. It is not ultimately for you. If it was, you would be weak and incomplete, because selfish motivation has no aloha. You take care of you for the ultimate purpose. So you can take care of others.

Airplane

"There's no reason to become alarmed, and we hope you'll enjoy the rest of your flight. By the way, is there anyone on board who knows how to fly a plane?" Elaine Dickinson, Airplane

"Oxygen and the air pressure are always being monitored. In the event of a decompression, an *oxygen mask* will automatically appear in front of you. To start the flow of oxygen, pull the mask towards you. Place it firmly over your nose and mouth, secure the elastic band behind your head, and breathe normally. Although the bag does not inflate, oxygen is flowing to the mask. If you are travelling with a child or someone who requires assistance, secure your mask on first, and then assist the other person."[6]

Ever wonder why you are supposed to, "secure your mask on first, and then assist the other person"? Because you need to take care of number one so you can take care of others. Get your mask on first! And then assist others. Get your mask on first, because you don't know what is going to happen next. There are a thousand events that can happen in a split second and you will be more prepared to take care of others if your mask is secure. Your kid sitting next to you might suffer for a few seconds, while you take care of you, but after those few seconds you will both be better off.

Here is the problem though. You are in that situation when the plane is malfunctioning for whatever reason. There is a sudden panic in the air. Maybe you feel the plane losing altitude or there is severe weather outside and the plane is being tossed around. You feel a pain in your ears and you realize the cabin is losing pressure. A few people scream as you embrace your sweet little girl on the seat next to you. You gaze into her grief stricken eyes. She thinks death is imminent and you assure her that everything is going to be okay. You can only sip the air, and oxygen masks suddenly fall from above.

Who in their right mind is going to put their mask on first? Think about it. Who is going to rip and push away from their little girl to put their own mask on first? Not Mama Bear. Not your wife on the best day of her life! Certainly not you! Is it the right thing to do? Heck yes it is (Napoleon Dynamite voice)! But you cannot possibly do it. Only a small percentage of people can actually follow this rule and do it right.

Ned Flanders and Mr. Rogers would do it. Anyone anal enough to follow instructions to the tee no matter what. Also pilots, flight attendants, and anyone who flies so much that the words, "secure your mask on first" have been imprinted on their brains and they have trained themselves for that actual situation. Service professionals like some firemen, EMT's, and military who know there is value in following the rules in spite of what their instincts tell them. Forest Gump would probably secure his mask first. Still, only a small percentage of people are going to follow that rule.

And therein lies the problem! You won't secure your mask first just like you will not take care of yourself first. Even though it is the right thing to do, your instincts are too strong and override what is right. It becomes habitual putting every task, every job, every person above yourself. Pretty soon you are the last person on your priority list. Because you don't take care of yourself first, you don't take care of yourself like you should or at all.

How to Take Care of #1

"I'm starting with the man in the mirror" MJ

Let me first give a shout out to the guy playing in two softball leagues plus works out for an hour and a half after work everyday and plays poker every Wednesday night. If you can manage all that, and your wife is good and you are spending quality time with your kid(s), then more power to you. But if you have a special needs kid and/or kids younger than high school, you have probably learned that those days are over. Or at least those days are on hold until kids get into high school and are loaded with schoolwork, sports, a job, friends, and extracurricular activities.

148

If you are that guy, you gotta let it go man. Take care of number one, but not only number one. Your window with a normal kid is so small. Your window with your special needs kid may not be so small, but any professional will tell you the early years are crucial. Take care of number one, but don't be selfish.

For the majority of you who work a full day and then come home to be with your families, I hear you. You might be tired and the kids want to play. Your kids need attention and it is a lot of work. Your wife has been going strong all day and needs a break. You have problems to deal with, assignments, your own chores around the house. The day ends and you have done nothing for yourself. The days roll into weeks and you look in the mirror one day and discover you are pale, aging, and fat.

Live to Outlive

"We never win because you are fat!" Esqueleto, Nacho Libre

Two thirds of men are fat. Cardiovascular disease is the leading cause of death for men 35 and older. Ah the statistics of fat men are plentiful and not much different than that of women and children. Here's to obese America! Oh, I should mention that men are more content being fat than women or children. That's us! We are just fine being fat. No problem, I am what I am right? WRONG!

The first action in how to take care of you, is physical exercise! Regular activity improves your quality of life. It makes you feel good about yourself and builds confidence. Exercise can have immediate and long-term health benefits. It will improve your health and reduce the risk of developing several diseases like type 2 diabetes, cancer and cardiovascular disease.

Physical exercise is the best way to take care of you. I am not here to give a health symposium. There are thousands of ways to get exercise and motivation. Find something that works for you and do it! Consistency is key! Get on some kind of program as small as it may be and stick to it.

Personally, I struggle with getting exercise. There are not enough hours in a day for me to get in a workout that I like. I love to surf, but that requires two hours of my time to get in a decent session. I would like to join any kind of sports league, but again, it's a two-hour commitment and often times happens in the evening when I am needed at home. However, a lot of leagues begin later when my kids are going or are in bed. I am too much of a wimp to stay up that late though. My body wakes up early no matter what time I go to sleep. I'm just wired that way. If you can do the 9:00PM basketball game without dragging the next day, you're on it.

So some days I get in a modest run or stop at the gym for an hour if I can squeeze it. But most days I cannot squeeze it. So I force myself to do 10 pushups before I go to bed. Last night I was so tired I rolled onto my stomach and did three girl pushups in bed. Does that even count? It does. One, because it is all about consistency. Do something everyday even though it's weak. Two, because I occasionally get in a weak workout I'm motivated to redeem myself and make up for it the next day. But that's me. I know me. I have my formula and I do what I've got to do to get it done.

You know yourself. Are you a complete slacker? Or are you in the minority and pretty fit? What's your formula? Don't have one? Figure out what you've got to do to get it done. Get a trainer or someone who will hold you accountable. Join a team so you have to show up on Tuesday nights. Today's the day. Figure it out right now. Make a goal to work out everyday even if it's a weak workout. Do what you've got to do to get 'er done.

The second action in how to take care of you is eating right. For my entire life I have believed that exercise was more important than eating right. Like most of you I subsist on a see food diet. I see food, and I eat it. But my neighbor and my spare tire have convinced me that I have been in the wrong for too long. So break out those fruits and veggies, give the red meat the day off today and the doughnuts for the month. Be a fit Dad! Be a healthy husband!

You have a child with a handicap. You do not have the luxury of letting your body fall apart like your brother. You are living the higher law. Of my three kids with special needs, one kid will need me to live as long and as healthy as I possibly can. Another kid,

I'm fairly confident will be fine on his own. And the other, I really don't know. But all three deserve two parents who will be healthy and living for as long as possible.

Your child, no matter what her issues are, deserves two parents to be healthy and around as long as she is. That's right! I said it! Live your life to outlive your child. Well, that is the saddest thing ever that a parent should bury his own child. Again, you are in a different world and you live by a different set of rules or lack thereof. Your kid may have a life expectancy of 9 or 89 years. It may not be possible to outlive your child. Does not matter! Plan and live to outlive your kid.

The third action in how to take care of you is laugh. Have fun for cryin out loud! All work and no play makes Daddy a dull boy. Nobody wants to hang out with a grump. So don't be one. Get out there and do something fun. When you come home after work, do what you need to do before you walk in that front door to be fun. Go cut it up with some buddies. Hang out with that guy who makes you laugh. When was the last time you laughed hard, really hard, from the belly?

The fourth and final action in how to take care of you is a free space. It is whatever you need. We are simple creatures who don't need much. Call it one of the cool things about being a guy. If you are high maintenance, you will soon discover that you cannot be that way with a special kid. You just can't. Your time is too valuable to your family.

Let me give you some examples of a free space. My relationship with God is important to me. So everyday I take a little time to read some scripture and do something spiritually uplifting. That's my free space. You may be an intellectual or a thinker who feels better when you stretch your mind and learn something new. You may like researching the latest galaxy NASA has discovered or a new species of frog in the Amazon. You may just need some time alone to think and process. You may like to read or have the ultimate collection of coins or the best saltwater fish tank in town.

Hobbies are a fantastic way to breathe life back into your soul. Are you a member of a club or organization that you enjoy? Are you building a chicken coup or playground in your back yard? Got a project or two in the works? How about a pet or two or twenty? Anything to give you purpose or allow you to gain some balance in your life. What about toys? It is so nice to blow off some steam behind a ski boat or blowing up a sand dune on your ATV.

Free space does not have to be a daily thing nor does it have to be one thing. I do some kind of treasure hunt or gold prospecting about once every six months. I fish, spear fish, play a round of golf, go rock climbing, and shake the cobwebs off my road bike about once a year. I like to accomplish something major like hike Mount Whitney or write a book about once every 5 years. These things challenge and fulfill me.

An added bonus to the four actions is that you can kill two or three birds with one stone. If I go surfing that takes care of getting exercise, doing something fun and often times it is a spiritual moment for me. If I can get a sitter and convince my wife to come, I can call it a date for the week. The possibilities are limitless

Let your kids have a cool dad who has or does something. Taking care of you means doing things that will benefit you. There are also a lot of mindless to bad ways to occupy your time. Is the screen sitter babysitting you? Unless you are gaming with your son or friends, you could be wasting a lot of time. Did you know couples who have a television in their room sleep less? It's true. You start watching something in the comfort of your own bed. You have all the intentions of turning off the TV after your program. But you start channel surfing and next thing you know you're up two hours later and have gained nothing except that you know who got voted off American Idol.

We have already talked about screen time. Use it in moderation. If you can't, then get rid of it. Do the activities that will give you benefits now and in the long run. What do you need? What will fulfill and prepare you for tomorrow. What makes you whole? Find your style. Make time for yourself without sacrificing time with those under your roof. Do your thing when it doesn't affect anyone. If that is not possible, do the best you can, but do something for you.

All Aboard

The last and perhaps most important ingredient in taking care of you is gaining the support of your partner. This can be a huge motivator if your wife supports and encourages you. Imagine her helping you get a workout in. Maybe she takes on a role like a coach. If your wife is like that, count your blessings.

For many of you gaining support is a huge barrier as a lot of women do not see the value in taking care of yourself. If Mama Bear knows you are down at Arnolds playing in the band with Richie, Ralph, and Potsie while she is has a messy house, can't get dinner on, and is wiping butts, you are not going to have a warm reception when you get home.

Unfortunately, man's solution to this is often times to simply not tell wife that you are at Arnolds. It is the easiest solution. What she doesn't know won't hurt her right? This is a slippery slope my friend! Do not withhold information. It is not right and will lead to worse decisions. Do not be dishonest or play games or justify a workout even if you really need to break a sweat and your wife just does not get it. Your relationship is built on trust and shouldn't be compromised if she does not support your stress relieving activity.

Instead, work on her. You can do it. You are a team! You got this. Here's a couple role plays just in case you need some ideas. Prep the subject with a fun date night or POG (Parents Only Getaway) or whatever you got. Remember timing is everything! Mood is everything! She must be in a good to great mood.

1. Hey (insert wife's pet name). I have a problem and was wondering if you could help me out. I feel like I have been aging at an accelerated pace in the last few months. I keep telling myself I am going to take better care of my body and lose some weight. Sometimes I start a fitness routine, but it doesn't last. Can you help me figure something out? I want to be here for you and the kids every day. I have to work

and sleep, so there is little time for much else? Should I wake up earlier? Ride my bike to work? Stop at the gym on my way home? What do you think?

2. Hey Sugar Pie Honey Bunch you know that I love you. I have gained 20lbs since we married 10 years ago. I know, I wear it well, right? But seriously, my metabolism has slowed down and will continue to slow. I am on pace to gain another 20lbs probably in the next 5-7 years. And then I will be that guy with his gut hanging over his belt. I need to change if I want to be around to take care of you and our kid. You know I have a hard time with food. If there are sweets in the cupboard, it is only a matter of time before they are in my gut. Can you please shop healthier? Maybe less junk food, processed foods, and more fruits and veggies?

3. Hey Shweetie-Pie-Shnookums, I am sorry I have been short-fused with the kids. Seems like I am getting a little more crotchety every day. You know what would really help me out? How would you feel if I went to my happy place for 20 minutes every now and then? Just me in the basement working on my erector set. Just me in the garage tinkering with my tools. Just me in my chair reading my Outside magazine. It really helps me unwind and puts me in a better place.

4. Hey Rockin' Baja Mama, you know that book you gave me to read about being a better husband and dad when you have a unique family like ours (that would be this book)? Well, the experts are saying I need to take care of me so I can be that husband and father that everyone around here deserves! They, the experts, suggest that once in a blue

moon I try something new or accomplish something big, like when I went on that cattle run with Mitch, Phil, and Ed several years ago. You know, check off something on my bucket list. Well, this would be a big sacrifice for you, but Little Joe and Hoss have invited me to ride with them on a 5 day off-road adventure. I'll never do the Baja 1000. This is a safe outing of just us guys out in the desert carving it up. What do you think?

Cinderella

My little girl's favorite story is Cinderella, big surprise I know. I've read it to her so many times I can watch a football game on TV and read her the book simultaneously without missing a word.

Cinderella got the laundry done, the floors scrubbed, the castle cleaned. She got her wretched stepsisters all dolled up and ready for the ball. She had no time for herself, but miraculously, the birds and the mice were able to finish her gown and she made it downstairs just in time. Once her stepsisters noticed the beads and sash that they had tossed out were on Cinderella's dress, they attacked her and tore the dress to shreds. Downtrodden, Cinderella goes out to the garden to be alone and cry. Despite being so cheerful and positive she proclaims that there isn't anything to believe in anymore. In short, she threw in the towel.

If the fairy godmother doesn't appear to save the day, what happens to Cinderella the next morning? Does she wake up on the right side of the bed, pull herself up by her bootstraps and attack the day with renewed hope? Maybe? But how long do you think she can last under those circumstances? At what point does she lose confidence? Constantly cooking and cleaning and sewing for a group of thankless people who order her around. At what point does she lose her self-esteem, become less pretty, and begin dishing out a bit of medicine of her own?

The only thing that saved Cinderella from becoming a miserable servant with an inferiority complex was her fairy godmother. With-

155

out her, Cinderella's dreams would have gone from being the princess to a possible appearance on the Jerry Springer Show where she could air out her sister's dirty laundry.

Sometimes, maybe even often, your wife gets treated like Cinderella. There aren't any birds or mice helping her do chores. I am pretty sure there is no fairy godmother coming to her rescue either.

Mission Impossible

Your mission, should you choose to accept it, involves repairing any damages caused by living like Cinderella for so long. Your woman's self worth must be recovered and enhanced. You see, it is one thing to convince you that you are number one. It is mission impossible for anyone to convince your wife that she is number one.

This is one chapter that applies to your wife more than it does for you! The same concepts and rules apply. Your wife must realize that she needs to train herself to secure her own oxygen mask before her children and before you. She needs to know that she is number one. If she does not take care of herself, she won't be around or as effective in taking care of others.

She must get physical exercise, eat right, laugh, and have a free space. You may and should select others to help. As always, should any member of your team be caught or killed, we will disavow all knowledge of your actions. This message will self-destruct in five seconds.

Tennis Anyone?

"You cannot be serious!" John McEnroe

My attempts at Mission Impossible were mediocre at best. We had three little boys and our Tyler was a mess. Life in our home was high stress and something had to be done. I knew my wife needed something outside of our home. She needed a release or a break. She needed to take care of number one. But Mama Bear has too much on her plate to worry about numero uno.

I tried reading to her at night. I offered to watch the kids so she could get away for a couple hours and do anything she wanted. She said, "All I want is for this house to be clean." And so I would clean. But nothing really changed as my wife burned the candle at both ends and rejected any suggestion I made.

Robin played tennis in college. Following the last match her senior year she put that racket down and didn't pick it up for five years. Another six months would go by before she dusted the racket off again, and play continued to be a rare event. During our difficult time when Robin really needed something, I suggested getting involved with the local tennis club. This was shot down repeatedly. There were a hundred reasons why she didn't want to play tennis or soccer or go to a fun event with some friends or do anything for herself.

One day I thought, I need to make a bold move. I knew I would end up in the doghouse, but I was in the doghouse all the time anyway. So why not take a chance. You know the definition of insanity right? Doing something the same and expecting different results. Well Mama Bear was not going to do anything different, so I took matters into my own hands.

I went to the local tennis club and signed her up to play on a tennis team. I spoke to the team captain and told her about Robin. She told me to have her at the courts Tuesday morning for her first match. I asked her to make the call. She was cool and agreed to do it. I was a nervous wreck worrying about that call and kept my head on a swivel in anticipation of recoil.

A couple days later Robin said, "I received a phone call today from someone instructing me I have a match Tuesday morning." The brilliant part of the plan is that Robin can't say no. She is too polite to say, I am sorry but my idiot husband did not have permission to sign me up for this. So I went to the doghouse and she went to play tennis.

Five years later she is still playing for the same club. Everyone is better off because of it and I am making fewer trips to the doghouse. We still have kids who are not in school at match time, so I watch the kids or we get a sitter or a friend. We make sacrifices. We do what we need to do.

Shelf Life

If there was a battle of the sexes, and a grocery store was the venue, men would not stand a chance. That playing field is listing heavily towards the dames. It doesn't matter how much time I spend in my local grocery store, I still cannot find things as fast as a woman who has never set foot in there before. Also, I overpay for things all the time. You should hear Robin when I get home. "You paid that much for this?...Did you look to see if this was available?...why didn't you..." I still make it out of there much faster than any woman who isn't late to something though. Figure that one out.

What I'm getting at is one day I was in a grocery store shopping for fruit. I'm thumping watermelon, sniffing pineapple and asking women if something was ripe and how can you tell. Women also know where everything is so no need to find an employee. The closest lady to you knows where everything is. In any case, I hate it when food goes bad. I am an avocado lover, but if those things go bad and I can't make guacamole, I am not a happy camper.

So in discussing freshness with this lady another lady chimes in and offers her opinion on whatever vegetable we were on. Sure enough another lady joined the discussion, but only to say, "that

158

guy over there is the best resource ever! He knows everything." It was an employee, so we waved him over. Sure enough he had an answer for everything. I asked him everything I ever wondered about the produce section. Where did everything come from? How much came from Mexico? When is it best to buy?

He knew the shelf life of everything in the store, even the junk food. Corn on the cob stays fresh for maybe a week, but a can of corn can go a couple years. I asked about everything I loved and saved the best for last.

You know when Adam and Eve partook of the forbidden fruit? I'm pretty sure it was a large ripe strawberry growing on that tree. The Bible says that it was desirable above all other fruit. Had to be a strawberry right? So I asked the expert, how long are those strawberries going to last. He said this afternoon. They got them in that morning and they will throw them out at the end of the day. WHAT! Those sweet delicious strawberries only last a day? What a heartbreaker.

Through the years, we have tried several remedies for Robin to take care of Robin. The best being tennis. The worst being, uh, ohhh, there are so many failures. But through this trial and error my wife has really learned to take care of herself. She is number one and she knows it. And believe me, I consider this one of my greatest accomplishments. She is busy as a bee, and is in fantastic shape. She feels great, looks great, and is so much fun! I'm gushing I know, but it would not be possible unless she knew she was number one.

As good as I have it at the moment, being number one is a continuous process. The self worth of a lot of women has a shelf life of a strawberry. Your wife may easily fall into that category. Her optimism, confidence, and self-esteem may be as sweet as a ripe red strawberry today, but expire tomorrow. It is fragile and must be continually edified and nourished because that shelf life is short. Even if your wife has the shelf life of a pineapple, it is still a daily process. Getting your wife to know that she is number one is great, but getting her to know it every day is a mission.

Rundown

1. Number One

   A. Who is number one? You are!

2. Airplane. Secure your oxygen mask first.

3. How to take care of number one

   A. If you already spend too much time on yourself, give it up. Time with your kids is too valuable and limited.

   B. Live to Outlive

      1. Physical exercise

      2. Eat right

      3. Laugh

      4. Free space

4. All Aboard. Must get the support of your wife!

5. Cinderella. Not so different from your wife.

6. Mission Impossible. Convince your wife that she is number one.

7. Tennis Anyone? Do what you've got to do.

8. Shelf Life. Your wife is a strawberry.

   A. Mission impossible is mission accomplished.

Priority Pyramid

This is my current priority pyramid. Over the years it has undergone several changes and facelifts. I have worked hard to get it to where it is now. Every so often I time and analyze my day to figure out if and how my pyramid is changing. Sometimes it is a good change and sometimes it is not. Nevertheless, it is a work in progress with a goal in mind.

You may be looking at this pyramid thinking there is so much more to life than what is represented. Try to put everything you do into one of the four tiers. I did not want to get too elaborate. If you volunteer at the soup kitchen or give some kind of service, that is for you. You can divide actions up. Do you go to church? Fix the toilet? Get the car serviced? You probably do that for everyone. Do you go to an unproductive Thing at the behest of your wife? Yea, you are doing that for your wife. If it doesn't meet your criteria and you cannot figure out where the activity goes, then don't do it. It is a waste of your time.

"He who every morning plans the transaction of the day and follows out that plan, carries a thread that will guide him through the maze of the most busy life. But where no plan is laid, where the disposal of time is surrendered merely to the chance of incidence, chaos will soon reign." — Victor Hugo

Work

Work is at the bottom of the pyramid because it is the least important. It is the by far the largest section because that is where most of my time is spent. It is also at the bottom because it provides a foundation for the rest of the pyramid. Without work, I could not support what is on top. Work provides security, stability, a challenge, and makes me a better man. It has always been on the bottom acting as the foundation. It was very small when I was unemployed and very large when I was working too much.

As important as this foundation is, I don't really like it. My goal is to make it more enjoyable and fulfilling. I do want to shrink the size and ultimately eliminate it. Don't get me wrong, my work is fine. The main reason I don't like it is because it takes time away from my children, my wife, and me. I am more happy, fulfilled, challenged, and refined working on my family then I am my work. Depending on your kids and their needs, you may be in the same boat. In a perfect world my pyramid should look like this.

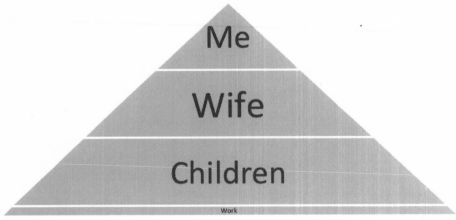

This is what I am working for. Can you see the work tier? It's a sliver at the bottom. Work is the least important and gets the least amount of my time. My kids are different kids and need more of my time. My wife and I are still on top, though I don't need that much time. Back to reality and my current priority pyramid.

In our world of special needs, it would be far better to be retired from work now while my kids are young, so I can focus on their growth and needs. The early years are so important and generally speaking require more care. Later in life they may not be around and not need me at all. Nevertheless, we need money and that foundation to live, and so I work.

Children

Children are next on the priority pyramid. I spend significantly less time with them than I do work. But as we have already discussed, this is not by choice. Give them everything you can especially in the early years. Your section of the priority pyramid could be smaller or larger depending on how many children you have and what their needs are. I have five kids and wish this tier was larger. You could have the same size section with one kid depending on what he requires plus how much time you have.

Sometimes I find the size of my work tier shrinking just enough to get by because my children need me more. Don't play around with this. Give your kids your time, but unemployment is not an option for you.

By the way, if you are looking for the "how to be a rad dad" section in this book, you won't find it. Well why not? After all, the title is "Keep It Together Dad," so it's a book about being a dad. Yes! However, the relationship a father has with his son or daughter in most cases comes quite naturally. Do you need someone to tell you that you need to spend time with your kids? You need to understand, nurture, meld with, love, show compassion, and be their best friend. Teach them, learn from them. There is no coaching required. He is your offspring. Nobody knows your kid better than his parents. If you need to hear that, then there you go. Just be a father. It is your natural responsibility and it's a fun and rewarding one.

Declaration

Everyone on your pyramid should know where they stand with one exception. No one needs to know you put yourself at the top. Many people will view it as being selfish. It can be selfish if you allow it, so be vigilant. You may need to tell your wife, but that is only to gain her support. No need to walk around telling everyone that you are number one and not them. Everyone thinks they are number one to you anyway, right?

My work knows I give them an honest day's labor. They also know they are at bottom of the ladder. They know this, not because I tell them they all suck, but, because I carry myself like a proud husband and father. I don't need to gush about my kids, although sometimes I'm sure I do. They all know I am going to the ballfield or home after work and not out with anyone I am not related to.

My kids know where they stand because I tell and show them all the time. They know I have to work so we can have a home and food on the table and the essentials. They also know I would much rather be with them than at work. I tell them and I show them.

They also know that Mommy towers over them on my priority pyramid. I have had the following conversation several times with my kids. It is usually around the dinner table when someone asks, "Dad, who do you love more, me or Mommy?" To which I reply, "Mommy, It's not even close." It is almost a game to them. A few weeks later in a similar setting, one of them will ask again. When they ask, I interrupt them before they can spit out Mommy, "Dad, who do you love most me or Mo..." Me: "Mommy, it's not even close. Now pass the peas please." And everyone laughs and mumbles, "Oh man!"

They know Mommy is queen. They know we are a team and that I support her and love her more than anyone one earth. They know there is no way they will ever be able to get one of us to take sides against the other. This is especially vital during teenage years as I am finding out. They see the way I treat her in our home and in public and there is no doubt that she is the most valuable person in the world to me.

164

You should hear the conversation before or after a POG (Parents Only Getaway). It usually goes something like this:

Kid: Dad, are you taking mom on a cruise again?

Dad: Yep, you want to see the ship?

Kid: Yes! Oh that thing is huge! Can I come?

Dad: Not a chance.

Kid: Why not!?

Dad: Because Mommy and Daddy need to go and spend time together without any kids. I love mommy, and I miss her. She spends so much time with you and every once in a while I take her away so I can have her to myself.

It is important they know I love their mother and that she is number one. That is why you don't need to tell your kids that you are really number one. This will only confuse them. When they complain about not coming on a POG, I usually point out a fun family vacation or two and explain the difference between that and a POG. Then I say, "When you have kids, you will do the same thing." And I know they will.

Wife

The next rung up the ladder is the best looking of the entire pyramid. You fell in love with her long ago and she means the world to you. If she doesn't, then her space on your pyramid is not right. Nurture that relationship and put her in the proper place.

Enough has already been said about your wife and why she nearly tops the pyramid. Your thoughts should be on your wife more than anyone. Remember the antecedent? Always be one step ahead of her if you can. What is she up to? What can I do to make her life easier? How can I make her know that she is number one?

She does not get the time that work gets nor what you devote to your children. But what she gets is quality time. She gets time where and when she needs it or as best you can. Take her out once a week. Take her on a POG once every 6 months or whatever you can do. Remind her why she married you on a consistent basis. You don't need to remind her that you are actually at the top of your pyramid, because she won't believe you.

Me?

Yes you! You are actually the ruler of your pyramid! You are number one. No one on your pyramid will believe you because they see you put your wife and kids on a pedestal. But in reality, it is you. You are number one. Funny how you are the most important but you get the least amount of time? How can that be?

I would love to sugar coat or spin this in a way that makes sense. But the reality is you get the least amount of time because there is no more time left for you! Well how can I be the high scorer if I get whatever time is left over? It's not like that. First, you are not taking leftover time. Your time for you is a priority, so take it. Second, and this puts it in perspective, <u>you require the least amount of time</u>. That's all.

Remember, you are a guy. You don't need all the time your wife and kids need. You are low maintenance and you figure it out. Remember, a lot of stuff just doesn't matter. You can get a laugh, exercise, be fulfilled, and feel good, without draining the clock. Many of you are thinking, what's the big deal? I feel great and I never have to think about doing something for myself. And that's fantastic. I feel like that all the time myself. In fact, it wasn't until I was in the trenches with my Tyler in the year from Hell, that the thought of taking better care of myself occurred.

For a few years, I wouldn't really think about taking better care of me until I was a grump or my fuse with my kids and wife was short. Now, I'm all about preventative maintenance. It's my own antecedent. Get out in front of it. Do what you've got to do and take care of numero uno.

166

Preventative Maintenance

This is my own routine. It changes constantly, but that is part of the fun. I get bored with the routine if it becomes just that, too routine. In any case, this is how I take care of me. First, the night before, I plan out the following day. If I am organized, I am productive and engaged throughout the day. I have my get busy list (to do list) ready to go. I put whatever I am dreading most at the top of the list. My Dad actually writes out the day in the past tense, as if it already occurred. He says when he sleeps his subconscious is working on it. Hey! Whatever works for you.

Second. I really enjoy eight hours of sleep. I am fine with seven, but eight is great. I know a lot of you haven't had eight hours of sleep in a long time. And some of you don't want or need that much sleep. I used to live off of less, but for now, I'm going for eight if I can get it. I am also, for the most part, early to bed early to rise. It's just how I'm wired. When I get my kids down for the night, I am not far behind. If I do stay up it's usually for my wife.

I am up early. Often times way too early. My friends and business colleagues kid me about receiving my emails at 4:00AM. I used to work out in the mornings, but it is the most productive time of the day for me. I get far more done in the morning than any other time. It's my hour! I own the morning! I read, think about what I need to think about, write, plan, work, etc. Two hours or more before anyone gets up, I am getting it done.

My work schedule is erratic, but I try to get a workout in usually around lunch. Occasionally, if time is on my side, I'll grab a surf, paddle, dive, or anything. I like to read, but rarely have time, so I listen to books in the car. It helps me zone out or get into a story and stir a little emotion in me. I call my brother or an old friend if I need a laugh. And that's it. I am priority number one, but taking care of me doesn't detract from anything or anyone else. Sweet.

The Rundown

1. Your pyramid is in a constant state of change. Work on it.

2. Work. It is the foundation but least important.

3. Children. Give them your time.

4. Declaration. Let everyone know where they stand.

5. Wife. Make her feel like she is #1. Quality time.

6. Me. You are king but require the least amount of time

7. Preventative Maintenance. Whatever works for you. Do it without detracting from anyone else.

POG

(Parents Only Getaway)

Let's go and see the stars
The milky way or even Mars
Where it could just be ours

Let's fade into the sun
Let your spirit fly
Where we are one
Just for a little fun
Oh oh oh yeah!

I want to get away
I wanna fly away
Yeah yeah yeah

Lenny Kravits, Fly Away

POG (pronounced like it is spelled... POG rhymes with hog) stands for two things. Both are awesome. The first is Passion Orange Guava, which became my favorite drink while attending college in Hawaii. The second is even better, *Parents Only Getaway*. Many of you think it is not in reach and will never happen. Others believe it may be years away. And still others have little to no desire to take one. What you need to understand is that POG is the gateway to the good life. It transcends all Valentines days, birthdays, and holidays. It supersedes any loving gesture, therapy, or family reunion. It is the pinnacle of dating your wife.

Most married men suck at dating. Add kids and it gets worse. Add a kid with special needs and you pretty much rule the suck pool of degenerate daters. But you have a different kid with different needs. And so you figure this is just one of those sacrifices you and

169

your wife make in light of your different circumstances. WRONG! There will be plenty of divergent sacrifices in your life. But ixnay on spending quality time with your wife *should not be one of them!* In fact it's just the opposite. Because of your diverse family, you and especially your wife need that time together more than anyone else.

Uncle Ed

My Uncle Ed passed away recently. This guy was something else. He had a Ph.D. in Mechanical Engineering, worked in the aero-nautical industry on such projects like the Space Shuttle, taught at a few colleges, started his own company, all of that. As a kid, my dad would tell us near death stories of Uncle Ed when he was in the military. He grew to legendary status for my brothers and me as we contemplated how Uncle Ed could still be alive.

As accomplished as he was, he would tell you that he is most proud of his family, and that his greatest accomplishments were being a husband and father. At my brother's wedding, they had that moment where they ask all the married couples to dance. You've seen it. The DJ says "if you've been married less than 5 years take a seat." Then a little later, he asks everyone married for less than 10 years to please sit down. And then 15 years and 20 and so forth.

When they got to 40 years, Uncle Ed and Aunt Pat were the only couple standing. They were still standing when the DJ hit 50! Then of course the DJ takes the microphone out to the middle of the dance floor and asks them what the secret of their success is. Without hesitation, they replied that they had been on a date every single week of their entire marriage. When Uncle Ed passed, they had been married 58 years. Aunt Pat still insists they never missed a week.

I would argue that his greatest accomplishment was taking his wife on a date every week for 58 years! Cal Ripken, Jr. Iron Man of baseball at 2,632 consecutive games played. AC Green Iron Man of Basketball at 1,192 straight games. And Brett Favre starts streak of 297 games is the longest all-time in the NFL. And now I give you the Iron Man of dating, my Uncle Ed at 3000 (give or take) consecutive weeks of taking his wife out on a date.

The Three Great Excuses

The value of a weekly date with your woman cannot be overrated. I am not going to dive into this and give you examples to convince you to regularly take out your wife. That's Marriage 101, and I'm not here to state the obvious. Being able to connect with your wife on a weekly basis without the little ones, is invaluable. You need that, and your wife needs it 10 times more than you. So why don't you do it?

No time, no money, no sitter. Ah yes, the three great obstacles of dating your wife. They are very real of course. I feel like I've been battling these three barriers since our first child came into our lives. Like most of you, I struggle with the weekly date. I'm not offering excuses, though we all have plenty. The big three excuses kick my butt too often and I need to get better.

Many of you struggle worse than me and may think the weekly date can't be done, at least on a consistent basis. Well I am here to tell you, men everywhere are pulling this off. I have a small handful of friends in my area who get it done every week and are reaping the benefits of it. One friend in particular is adamant about it. He went from rarely dating to always dating and subsequently zero to hero. He has made it a priority. Every Thursday night the sitter comes over at 7:00. They never call her. She knows it is set in stone and if she can't make it, she'd better let the couple know.

If I tell him I've got one ticket to his favorite sports event, he passes. Biggest work deadline of the year is looming? He puts it aside. Maybe a sick kid might keep them at home. But if that happens, they still set time aside for each other and have dessert on the back porch or play a board game or something non-routine. It is all a matter of making it a priority.

No time. **MAKE TIME!** You don't need much. Set aside a time every week and don't deviate from it! If you absolutely cannot make it, don't cancel! Reschedule, and ask your wife if she'll go out with you the following night. Never cancel, only reschedule for another night that week. Maybe there is an event Saturday night. And so you reschedule. Don't go too long without digging deep and making it special. If you can do that, good on you mate. But the goal here is consistency. What you do should be the least of your worries. Take the time to **MAKE THE TIME.**

No money. This is the worst excuse ever! Hello! You are dating your wife. She knows how much money you make. There are a thousand fun things to do that cost no money. Shake the cobwebs out of that brain of yours and exercise the creative juices. No money? Give me a break!

No sitter. I feel you on this one. For you, the dad of a special kid, this is a different animal. So many of you have not been on a date with your wife in months or years. Maybe you are able to spend time together alone, but it is always within the walls of your home. You're a good dad, so you watch the kids and let your wife take off. She needs the down time. But the two of you haven't been out together for a long time and you don't see it happening in the future.

Your child requires constant care from you or your wife. Or maybe that is not the case, but mama bear won't trust anyone to watch your kid or you're too shy or embarrassed to ask someone. There may be one or no persons your wife will trust with the care of your special kid. Only you know your situation. But let me offer this.

Take a chance! If your kid has a professional caretaker during the day, figure something out. If your child goes to school, have your wife meet you for lunch. If work is too far for your wife to travel, work something out. If both of you work or other kids are involved, day time dating may not be in the cards. In which case you'll have to focus on evenings and attempt to conquer every couple's greatest obstacle, FEAR OF THE SITTER, which we will discuss momentarily.

King of Things!

The longer you have a kid with special needs, the more you will be exposed to programs and organizations and as we discussed earlier, THINGS! We have already talked about Things and that many of them will not be worth your time, effort, and money. There is however, a Thing out there that is so fantastic, so awesome, it cannot be contained. And that is................wait for it............. RESPITE! Respite is free babysitting! Whoever invented Respite truly knows the value of keeping families together and strong.

School, therapies, lectures, and all those programs for your child are great, but Respite is king of the Things! In California Respite is a program the Regional Center contracts through the YMCA. The YMCA has a list of qualified baby sitters or you can get your own! You can even get a parent or relative! All they have to do is go through the training and background check and next thing you know, you've got a sitter you trust coming over every Wednesday night and getting paid for it. And it isn't coming out of your pocket.

Respite and programs like it are the single greatest Things for kids with disabilities. Many people may question that. But it is absolutely true because it nurtures and strengthens the very foundation of the family. The couple that dates regularly is far less likely to split and far more likely to love. The more love between husband and wife, the stronger foundation and family bonds, and everyone under your roof prospers.

Alaska Brown Mama Bear

In anticipation of our first born turning one year old, I planned our first POG ever. Babysitter, my mom, was all set to go. We had recently moved across the country back to our hometown. We were crashing at my parents place while looking for a home. So my mom and our baby were very familiar with each other. Flights, trains, lodges and activities in America's last frontier were all arranged. All systems go.

Funny thing happened when we stepped onto the plane. Our one year old was with us! Well, I love that little guy. He was just adorable. Everywhere we went he was the main attraction, especially since there are thousands of grandmas who visit Alaska every summer. We brought a backpack to carry that kid and took him on hikes, on the trains, and even rented bikes with a trailer. He saw moose, bears, all kinds of wild life, and the most beautiful scenery imaginable. We really had a good vacation.

Looking back on that Alaska vacation a year, five years, ten years later, am I glad we took our 12 month old baby? NO WAY JOSE! Is my wife glad we took him? Nope. It wasn't a memorable trip for the baby. Although he can tell his friends he went to Alaska, he doesn't remember a thing. Had we left him in the safe care of grandma, we would have hiked more, adventured more, experienced more, had way more sex, and devoted more time to each other.

We carried twice the luggage, changed diapers, fed the baby, got him his naps, and worried about him everywhere we went. We should have been running free, getting caught in the rain, drying out by the lodge fire, going to shows at night, sleeping in, and doing anything we wanted to do whenever we wanted to do it.

We were there in late September and got to experience summer, fall, and winter all in the same week. At the conclusion of our trip, I'll never forget, sitting in the hot tub of this beautiful Princess Lodge overlooking the Nenana River and picturesque Denali National Park. The first snow of the season began to fall and accumulate on this setting. The heat of the tub, the chill of the air, the tingle of the feathery snowflakes, the music of the river, and the graphic altering panorama of the creator's canvas put me in sensory nirvana. It was a moment in time that I'll never be able to duplicate.

The only thing I wanted was to share this rare event with my wife. So I jumped out of the tub and ran soaking to our cabin. I opened the door ever so quietly to my wife who was on the bed struggling to get an overtired baby to sleep. She wasn't going anywhere. It was the microcosm of the entire trip. A good family vacation could have been an epic POG. But Mama bear could not 'bear' the thought of leaving her cub with grandmamma bear.

Look, before you get all agro over this, I get it. Not many women will leave their 12 month old baby and go on vacation. I get that. When I planned the POG I knew there was a strong possibility Jr. was coming along. Truthfully, it would have been difficult for me to leave him. It doesn't matter. We still made the wrong decision.

174

So how old will your kid be when you leave her for a week? Is two years old okay? How about three? or five? How about leaving your child for a weekend when he is five years old? Is that reasonable? What about leaving your six year old for a two hour date with your wife? Here is what I am getting at.

RESPITE, the king of all Things, is far too underutilized. An unbelievable amount of people qualify for respite or similar programs and don't take advantage of it. Your sisters-in-law, wife's BFF, and others have offered to watch your kid(s), but you just won't do it. Why? This is a debacle. Here are the top three answers to that question. It may not be one or the other. Like us, you may have problems with two or three of these.

1. Pride. You are not going to take charity! You will pay for your own sitter! The problem with that is that most of the time you don't. You are going to need all kinds of help if you are the father of a special kid. Let that pride go, it won't do you any good.

2. Shyness. So many special needs families just hunker down, become anti-social and reclusive. You get comfortable indoors doing your own thing and just don't want to bother anyone. Your little world becomes smaller and smaller with outlets and resources becoming more scarce. This environment breeds problems and you might need a trip to the loony bin eventually.

3. Mama Bear and Fear of the Sitter. Mama Bear just can't tear herself away. That cub is her responsibility and she's going to stay with that offspring until the bitter end. She does not trust anyone, as no one will look after her kid like she does. No sitter, even if it's a relative, will understand what her child needs.

175

What if something happens! Not sure what the best answer is on this? Some couples rip the bandaid off and escape for a night or two when it is too soon. Then mama bear worries all night and that's no fun, plus she won't do it again. Personally, we took baby steps. A 30 minute date sitting in our car down the street slowly turned into a 60 minute walk close by. Then a picnic at the neighborhood park, all the while with our cell phones turned to the highest volume waiting for the call that Tyler had punched the sitter, cracked his head open, was receiving CPR, and had contracted the Ebola virus. When disaster doesn't strike and a little consistency develops, you might just find yourself going to the next Stones concert.

POG Heaven

"Soaking it up in a hot tub with my soul mate." Uncle Rico, Napoleon Dynamite

After you get a passing grade in "Dating With a Special Needs Kid 101," you may enroll in POG Heaven. Your ultimate goal is to master this course. It isn't any harder, just requires more time, is more fun, and soooo worth it! I mentioned before that Parents Only Getaway (POG) is the gateway to the good life. It absolutely is. The POG is the ultimate in couple's therapy. This is where you completely decompress. Where all troubles and worries are left behind. Egos, malice, hurt feelings, and mama bear are nowhere to be found. Stress and pressure simply melt away and it becomes easy to remember why you married your wife. More importantly, it will hopefully remind her why she married you.

This is your time to devote yourself to you and your wife. There are no kids, work, school, church, nor any responsibilities of any kind. It's just the two of you, like it was before you created any messes, I mean kids. Please leave the cell phones and gadgets behind. Prepare to unclench everything in your world and release the tension from every fiber within. You are able to laugh uncontrollably deep from the gut. You laugh so hard that if you have anything in your mouth it will come out your nose.

The battle has ended for the moment, and you may recharge your batteries and learn from each other. There is no hustle or rush or anger. I have a good friend who took his wife on a weekend POG to a mountainous area not far from his home. His mother-in-law insisted on the outing as she knew they were at each other's throats. As they drove up the mountain, they could not remember why they were so mad at each other. All of a sudden looming problems were non-existent.

It doesn't take long before both of you have your guard down and you can discuss anything without a hint of offence. Intimacy is restored and sex is rejuvenated. All the love and affection your wife pores out on your children suddenly has no place to go. And so it drenches you. You return the sentiment and the two of you sleep in the middle of the bed, right where that lump is on your bed at home.

You sleep for more hours, get more exercise, read a book, play games, do activities you normally would not do. Maybe you attend an event where your mind is stretched, learn a new skill, or who knows what? The sky is the limit. You are feeling so good, you might even try yoga.

Plopped down on a 14 foot couch contemplating trivial matters, your wife chooses to curl up next to you. Fondness reaches honeymoon levels and you find yourself involuntarily rubbing her feet! It just comes naturally, without thought, without intentions, you are rubbing feet. And then it dawns on you. This woman really is your best friend.

By the end of your POG, you are so physically relaxed and emotionally empowered that confidence has no boundaries. Both of you have decided to change some things around your home and live a little differently. You may have even set some goals. Your marriage is stronger than ever as the two of you are a formidable team! The foundation of your family is strengthened and your resolve to live life happier and healthier is cemented in the knowledge that you have your wife's unconditional love and support. What feels better than this, is that you've got her back too.

POG-ing Made Easy

Your Personal and Detailed Guide to the Good Life

If you spend too much time thinking about a thing, you'll never get it done.

Bruce Lee

All right! You heard the man! If you're not going to listen to Bruce Lee, than who are you going to listen to? You are not going to think about this 'Thing' any longer! You are a DOER! Bust out your preferred internet device and a pad of paper right now! I know you know how to book a vacation, but I have a few nuggets you haven't thought about. Plus you are more likely to get it done if you follow these instructions in order.

You won't be able to get it completely done in one sitting, unless you have already done the legwork or you have a lot of time right now. Also, I'm not going to make you book a 10 day trip to Tahiti, although I might. You can do a one nighter if that's what you can do. The point is to get something down, something on the horizon you and your wife can look forward to. But you will not simply read through this. You will do this! And you will do this with me, because I am over-due myself.

1. Formulate. First thing you need to realize is that planning a POG is FUN! As you begin to formulate in your mind the where, when, who, how, process, your blood will pump and your mind will race. PLEASE NOTE, the most important thing you do in every step, is to cater to your wife. You know her. What does she want? Will she go for this? How are you going to present and go about all this to bring her on board? Are you 'Formulating'? Good, I am formulating too.

2. Get a Sitter. The second step is quite possibly the most difficult, especially if you are just starting out. It is no longer difficult for me, for a couple reasons. One is that both my

178

mom and my mother-in-law totally rock! Do you know why they rock? Because they watch my kids! Does your mom think she's a rockin' grandma? Well, she's not unless she watches your kids *if she is capable.* Watching your kids is the best gift any Grandma can give bar none. No grandma on earth can claim they rock unless they watch their grand-kids! End of discussion.

You know that guy who goes out of his way to thank every man and woman who has served in the military? I thank them and show my appreciation of course, but this guy stops them when they walk by and sincerely thanks them for their service to our country. You know that guy? Well that's my dad. Everywhere he goes he's thanking our men and women in uniform. Well I am that guy when it comes to grandmas. If I know of a lady who is about to fly somewhere to watch her grandkids for a week, I am all over that. If I talk to a woman and find out she watches her grandkids so the parents can take a POG, I am gushing with appreciation and thanking her for her service. I tell them they are rockin' Grandmas and that I am going to submit their names for the Rockin' Grandma of the Year award.

Several years ago I picked up the phone and had the following conversation with my mom. I then dialed my mother-in-law and had the same conversation.

Rick: Hey uh, you know... there are 52 weeks in a year.

Grandma: yeah?

Rick: Could you please give us just one of those weeks every year? Your grandkids love you to pieces and you are so good with them.

Rockin Grandma: Sure

Rick: You don't know how much Robin and I appreciate this! especially since you know our kids are different. To be honest, it takes a toll on us sometimes, and a Parents Only Getaway, really, really helps us more than you can imagine.

So I committed both my mom and mother-in-law to giving us a week every year. That's two weeks a year for a POG! Sometimes we take it and sometimes we don't. Currently, one of our rockin' grandmas has been living in Japan for six months and will be there for another 18 months. Therefore she won't be watching our kids anytime soon. That's okay. Before she left I asked some siblings if they'd do it and all systems are a go if we need it.

Rick, aren't you afraid you are putting your siblings out? That's a pretty big favor you are asking. You dump your kids at your brother's house and you might get home and find that your relationship is tarnished for life. I used to worry about that, but now, it doesn't concern me at all. Here's why. If I was worried, I'd do a one nighter or whatever I felt comfortable with. Instead of being tarnished, most likely our relationship would be enhanced.

Ever watch your niece or nephew for a day or two or longer? Even if that kid was a complete brat, you still have made a bond there. He'll grow out of being a brat at some point and you'll be able to tell him what a brat he was at the family Christmas party years later. Everyone will laugh and you will be his favorite uncle for life. Yes, it is a big sacrifice watching your sibling's kids, but sacrifices bring blessings.

This is an extreme example, but when I was two years old and my little brother was 6 MONTHS OLD! My parents drove to Phoenix AZ and unloaded us at....... you guessed it, UNCLE ED STRIKES AGAIN! My parents jumped on a plane and toured Europe for... .....wait for it......... 6 WEEKS! Even in the heightened free-range parenting days of the 70's, this was extreme and maybe even unheard of. I don't really know because I was little and don't remember it. In fact, I don't remember anything about that 6 weeks I spent with my cousins. But they do. They were mostly teenagers and took care of us along with Aunt Pat of course.

Over the years I have seen those cousins rarely. And despite an age gap of maybe 7 to 17 years with them, and only seeing them once every 3-4 years, there is definitely a bond there stemming from that time we stayed with them. Even now, almost 40 years later, they talk about that time like it was last week. The stories have gotten old for *only* me and my brother of course, but apparently I loved to torture the cat, was the victim of several pranks including the old look in the hose nozzle until water comes gushing up your nose, and on, and on, and on.

Oh, there was a barf fest when everyone got sick, and one trip to the hospital because I threw something at someone's head and stitches were needed. Hey, it was all good then and all good now. I don't think I'd really know those cousins at all had it not been for that time we spent with them. And I'm sure I have a special place with Uncle Ed and Aunt Pat since they took care of me for that time.

So get on the phone right now and commit your mother and/or mother-in-law to watching your kids. If they are not capable, go with siblings. If they are not capable, try friends. If they are not capable, find the professional nanny or sitter you trust. If you can't afford that, there are rockin grandmas everywhere who would do it even though you are not related! I personally know several RG's who would watch our kids if we needed it. You know why they would do it? Because they are from the old school when you did things like that and people were not as selfish with their time and talents as they are today. And they love it. For many, it gives them purpose and makes them feel great as they are part of little lives.

Do you know what my mom said to me? Talk about being blessed. My mom is in her 70's. She's had a number of ailments including a hip replacement. Recently, she was telling me how good she feels. Then she said, "I am in good health because I watch your kids." Chew on that for a bit.

I speak freely about it, but truth is I am not comfortable asking anyone except my own mom to watch my kids. I am sure you are not comfortable asking anyone either. You figure your wife will do it, and maybe she will. BUT, unless it is her own mother, her comfort level asking someone could be worse than yours. This is one of the reasons this is such a difficult task. But the POG MUST GO ON! So ask! Share your adorable kid(s). Let them gain the

181

blessings that come from giving love and protection and service to a good family. It's all good.

What is the downside? It does not hurt to ask. If your brother cannot do it, then he'll tell you so. No biggie. If he, or anyone feels like, "whoa! that was rather audacious of him to ask me to watch his kids." Then he needs to pull the stick out of his butt and realize that trusting him with the care of your family is the ultimate compliment. That's on him or whomever might entertain that sentiment. You are going out on a limb with this request and most family and friends will recognize and respect that, whether they can care for your kid or not.

Your wife may or may not have all kinds of criteria for a sitter. Your standards on the other hand are considerably under par. The only thing you should ask yourself is, will this person protect my family? And that's it. If you can match your wife's criteria, then good on ya' mate. But that person may not exist, ergo, you ain't going anywhere.

Lets say cousin Eddy is the only relative you could get to watch your kids. He pulls his Winnebago up to your home and you can already tell the neighbors are offended. He and his drooling oversized dogs enter your house smelling toxic. You give him the schedule for the week, emergency numbers, some training, and off you go.

Seven days later you return home to find your kids wearing the same thing they were wearing when you left. Turns out Cousin Eddy is on a water conservation kick and he discouraged watering the plants, laundry, showering, dishes, or flushing toilets. Your little girl looks up at you and says, "if it's yellow let it mello, if it's brown flush it down Daddy." The house smells like Eddy and his dogs and there are pizza boxes from every night of the week stacked in the kitchen. The kids were late to school every day and there is a message from the principal on your wife's voicemail.

This is your worse case scenario and pretty much never happens, unless cousin Eddy really is your cousin. Your wife freaks out and says we never should have left. But it takes one day to air and clean the house, pump some nutrition into the kids, and put out the fires. Your wife cools down and you lie in bed looking at pictures you just downloaded from your week in POG Heaven. You laugh, talk, and realize the bonds, memories, and sparks of the week cannot be undone from the chaos you came home to. This is affirmed moments later when your wife curls up next to you and asks where the two of you might go on your next POG.

Need more inspiration on the sitter? There is a good family movie called Bedtime Stories. Watch it with your family. Your kids will love it. Courteney Cox plays a single mom who has to leave town for a few days. She exhausts all avenues to find a sitter, and reluctantly calls her never present brother, played by Adam Sandler, to watch her kids. In the end, the estranged Adam Sandler saves the day, falls in love, and has an unbreakable bond with his niece and nephew and consequently with his sister. It is a movie, yes, but these attachments do happen when you go on a POG. Probably not like they happen in this movie, but they happen none the less.

Exhausted all resources? Dig a little deeper, reach out. You may have to farm them out to different places or have a tag-team network of sitters. I know I don't need to say this, but for some of you numbskulls, use good judgment. No shady characters to watch your kids. Yes, cousin Eddy is a bit shady, but you know what I mean. Kids must be kept safe! Okay! Got your sitter? I do! Starting to get stoked now!

3. Money changes everything (Cyndi Lauper singing voice). Money has always been and will always be one of the leading factors of divorce. Don't let it be for you! It is also a leading factor in failed POGs for this one reason; if you spend $5000 *that you do not have* on an elaborate POG, it will come back to bite you. You are raising a family that will have all kinds of extra expenses associated with your special kid. You need to be financially responsible.

Going into debt or more debt for a POG is a bad idea. I'm not saying don't go if you have debt. Almost all of us have it. You just need to be smart about it. You can do a POG and spend little to no money. Money will factor into all the POG decisions you make. Are you paying for a sitter? How much do you leave the sitter to spend on the kids? Where will you go? How will you get there? Where will you stay? Where will you eat? What activities will you do? Money, money, money, money, money (For the Love of Money (apprentice voice)).

For all things money, I strongly recommend Dave Ramsey. It's good economic horse sense that you really cannot argue with. He'll have you paying everything off, getting out of debt, and an envelope you can label POG, where you put cash away for that purpose. I do have an account for POG's and family vacations, though it is not in a white envelope in my drawer.

I spend on our POG what is in that account and nothing more. Spending more means that it will be in the back of my mind while on the POG, and having that hanging over you will make you sad. And as my teenager says, "Don't be sad. Because sad spelled backwards is das. And das is not good (German accent)."

There are plenty of things to do that require little to no money on any budget. Robin and I just got a free night in a Marriott downtown from a Cerebral Palsy organization. They include parents of kids who have Down Syndrome, so we scored. They also gave us $50 for a sitter! Double score. Network with parents of disabled kids in your area and look for things. You might have something like that free night sitting under your nose. There are several programs and charities I would like to be part of or start. Getting POGs for parents of special needs kids tops my list. Stay tuned.

Robin and I have camped several times. We have stayed in homes of relatives and friends when they were there, and not there. We have even slept in a van down by the river. Well, maybe not down by the river, but yes, in the back of our minivan. I rack up hotel points on my credit cards when I travel. There are no more really good hotel programs as they have all doubled or tripled the amount of points needed for a stay, but it still might be worth it.

Your wife might not camp or go cheap. And you may have some extra work to make it presentable to her. Or she might be a total trooper and say, lets just get out of here, jump in the car and go where the wind blows us. The point is to get away. If a week at the

Shangri-La Hotel Paris is in your budget, good for you. If not, no worries, just get away together. A day, a night, a weekend, go for it. Whatever you can do. Just do it. Got dough set aside for your POG? Yep! Check yourself. You may need to shorten or adjust the getaway, or save a little more money.

4. Who is going? The purpose of the POG is for you and your wife. It is your time to be together and focus on each other. If you have not been on a POG in a while or ever, don't even think about inviting others. However, there are times and places, when bringing another couple, or two, or five, is beneficial. Cutting loose, laughing, conversing, catching up, supporting with friends can be a major plus to a POG if the circumstances allow. Accommodations away from everyone is always recommended and make sure you keep it about your team. That's why you are there.

Steer clear of any friends or relatives who have even a hint of a downside. Don't invite Noah and Allie. They fight occasionally and nothing ruins a POG like a couple's quarrel. You don't want your wife consoling Allie because she's mad at Noah. Do invite Ricky and Lucy. Lucy makes you laugh so hard you might need to bring an adult diaper. Don't invite Peeta and Katniss. That is way too much drama. Do invite Han and Leia. They will be the ones insti-gating the canopy zip line tour and shark cage dive. Maybe some of their awesomeness will rub off on you too. Made the invite list? I got mine.

5. How are you going to present this to your wife? Alert, Alert, Alert! Does your wife like to be surprised? Does she want to be swept off her feet? Will you need to talk her into it? Should you come clean early on and plan everything to-gether? Does she want to plan it? And when do you do all of this?

Personally, my wife usually does not want to plan. Part of the fun is she doesn't want to make any decisions. Conversely, I like making decisions and figuring out what we are going to do and when. I get to mind surf the POG before it happens. Having said that, our last POG was a one nighter for my birthday. She planned everything and kept it a surprise. She also hit it out of the park, so we may do a roll reversal again. Presentation ready? Bueno.

6. When to go. Don't get greedy on this! If you find a time that you, your spouse, and the sitter can do it, then all systems go. If that isn't a big deal and you have freedom in that area, do what you think your team needs. Robin and I have done spur-of-the-moment, last-minute deals. In recent years, we prefer to book months in advance. We do that so we have something to look forward to. But to each his or her own. The important thing to do is book it! Commit to it, and don't waver. Roger that. Setting date now.

7. Throw money at it. I know we have talked about money, but this is a different subject. You must pay for the vacation when you book. Do not get on a payment plan. Do not put a deposit down. Do not purchase trip insurance or anything that will give you a refund if something suddenly comes up. It was a bad excuse for Marsha Brady, and it is a bad excuse for you. Everything on God's green earth will suddenly come up before your POG. Expect it.

Throwing non-refundable money at it from the get-go shows you are committed and that nothing is more important than taking your wife away. Honestly, and this goes with number seven above also. Your family is special. It is sacred. Strengthening that family with a getaway is a wonderful thing. You should anticipate every negative force in the cosmos to take a stab at ruining your plans.

That guy at work who dishes out assignments chooses the worst possible time. Your mother-in-law suddenly has cold feet about watching your kids. A death in the family happens. Your kid suddenly requires more of your time and is getting into trouble at school. Negative energy is everywhere. Your wife is upset and the timing is all wrong. You interpret all this to mean that you are not supposed to go. "Horse Hocky!" (Colonel Potter, *Mash*). Man up! Very few things are more important than taking your wife away on a well deserved vacation.

Be determined and go. That's why you throw non-refundable money at it! So you have to go. This is the ultimate step. You throw money down and there is no turning back. You are standing on the beach and the captain is about to order the ship burned. Credit card out, entered, and confirmed! I am officially going and feeling so good. Go ahead and burn that ship. No turning back for me. How about you? Come on man! Don't be a wimp! Throw down that card and make a bold statement. You are going!

8. The basics. Where are you going? What will you do? Activities? Interests? Put yourself in your wife's shoes. What does she want to do? Remember you are a guy, so this stuff doesn't really matter to you. Chances are however, since you are married to each other, there have to be some common interests.

I really lucked out because over the years Robin has really developed a love for scuba diving, and I am totally down with that. Robin is also a warm water/weather person. So generally, our POG's are spent embracing the tropics, diving, surfing, immersing ourselves in a different culture, and exploring. So there you go. Find or develop common interests and all the basic questions are easy and fun to plan.

I don't know about you, but I just spent way too much time planning this section. It was really fun though. I feel like I'm already there. You got this?

9. Important things to do on your POG.

A. Take umpteen pics and vids! You will need them in the future. Remember, you are all about creating memories. The camera is the key. And use a real camera and not your phone. It's not that your phone doesn't take great pics, it's that you should not have your phone unless it is unavoidable. I don't remember my wife ever saying we took too many pictures. You can delete them anyway. But on several occasions we both felt we didn't take enough or any. Capture as much activity on film as you can. You don't need to go crazy with multiple pics of the same event, get a variety. Taking multiple pics of the same thing might slow you down. Don't let taking pics slow you down.

B. Decompress. Robin and I POG sometimes with my uncle and aunt. Uncle Rob is a veteran vacationer and has taught me a few secrets over the years. Every time we get to our destination, I'm pumped and ready to go, go, go! He on the other hand sets aside the first day as a day of decompression. I had no desire to sit around all day until my wife stuck me on a poolside chaise lounge, threw a book in my hands, and told me not to move.

An hour later I was totally into my book. I listen to books in the car, but rarely read for pleasure and had forgotten what it's like to get into a good book. An hour later, I took a dip in the pool. An hour later food came by then I took a nap. An hour later I am sunk into my towel filled lounge chair that has become my bed. I am unwilling to move much and tell my wife my body feels weird. She explained that I was now relaxed, and that it felt weird because it was foreign to me.

Take at least a day and let your body and mind uncoil from the busy life you lead. You may not think you need it until you force yourself to chill for a while. Before you know it, you have reached a state of zen and all is well in the universe. Get a massage, let the rubber band retract, eat good food, breathe the air, do some yoga, and *stretch*. Most importantly, make sure your wife is unwinding with you. Send her away for a pedi and some extra pampering. She'll bring you a poolside barbeque bacon burger on her way back so you still don't have to move.

C.   Create Memories! Do something different. Be adventurous. Attend a meeting in another language or take a pottery class. Get to know the locals. Do something you haven't done in years like rolling down a hill. Do service for someone. Do some cartwheels on the lawn and soak some tourists with your patented cannonball. Work out. Just because you are on vacation doesn't mean you shouldn't push yourself physically or mentally. Cut loose!

D.   Dote on your wife. Give her everything she needs physically, mentally, sexually, and emotionally. Give her your time and *attention*. Cook for her. Make something for her. Think about what she does for everyone on a daily basis. Make her feel like the woman she really is. Self-esteem is so fragile, especially for women. Don't let your wife have any doubt as to her self worth. Compliment her and build her up. She is amazing! And she is your queen so polish her crown.

E.   Communicate. Don't ruin a great vacation by bringing up any problems. Mule fritters! (Colonel Potter *Mash).*

189

The whole point of a POG is to strengthen the family by entrenching the heads of the house. You're a guy, so most to all the stuff your wife does that bothers you is long gone. However, she might have some items to get off her chest. Let her release the baggage. Be receptive to it. In fact, you should instigate it. Start with this, "Honey, during this trip, I've been thinking about my life and some changes I need to make. I know I've got plenty of things to work on. But can you please tell me two things I can do to be a better husband and father?"

Your guard is down. Her guard is down. You are both relaxed and having fun. Take the time to work on communication. Talk about changes that need to happen. Talk about home and when you should discuss things post POG. Where do you stand with each other? How good is your relationship and what can you do to strengthen it. If you have something to say, now is the time to say it. What supports do you need and when? Same goes for her.

This is your time, recommit to each other and resolve differences. Get rid of the garbage and nurture the marriage. Build on what you have already established. There may be hurtful words said, but this is the best time to not be offended, to get over it, and to move on. *"Hallucinate, Desegregate, Mediate, Alleviate, Try not to hate, Love your mate, Don't suffocate on your own hate, Designate your love as fate" INXS, Mediate.*

Don't discuss your kids on your vacation. "Pig Feathers!" (Colonel Potter, *Mash*). Take time to discuss your children, in detail, one at a time. How are they doing in school, sports, extracurricular activities, therapy, treatments, diet, friends, wants, and needs. This not only is a great team building exercise, but a fantastic time to discuss and plan alternative measures. Now that the two of you have reached a zen-like state and the great beyond is becoming clearer every day, what better time to receive inspiration or revelation regarding those people most important to you.

F. Leave the cell phone, tablet, laptop, and all gadgets behind. Look, I get it. You have to check your email every morning and night. You have to make an occasional call. You have to take care of business. The problem is that if it's there, you are so used to using it, you will involuntarily massage it instead of your wife's feet. All of a sudden, you are bored and it becomes increasingly important to check your email. While you are there, you might as well check the news and scores and, whoa! Check out this video posted on Facebook!

Think your wife doesn't know why you haven't joined her poolside yet? Think she doesn't? You get me on this? Do you really have the discipline to only check email and calls once and not let it bog you down and take your time? Leave the gadgets at home. It will do you good. The same goes for your wife if you can swing it. But there is one exception. If you need to be accessible to the caretaker(s) of your special needs kids, then you had better be available. Just have your wife's phone ready. Not yours.

G. RAD (Required Attention Diversion). You need to leave the world behind mentally. Work issues, family drama, children, whatever occupies your world needs to be put on the back burner. Actually, it shouldn't be allowed on the stove. Do activities that force you to focus on something else. A puzzle or an engaging book can put your mind in another world. A board game, a run, a massage or whatever gives your brain a reprieve is what you're

191

looking for. If your wife is homesick for her kids, go radical and stick her on a zip line or go skiing.

H. Goooooooooooooaaal (Latin soccer announcer voice). Robin and I have dear friends who have a 13 year old special needs daughter. They just had a four hour IEP meeting that they could not finish. So they packed on another two hours a few days later to wrap things up. It did not end well. She has Turner's Syndrome plus something else. The school district is currently paying for her at a non-public school. Our friends are trying to move her back into public school without much success. But I digress.

This couple recently took their first ever Parents Only Getaway. He had a business trip to Europe. They found a sitter and she went along. Results were off the scale. And so I would say to our friends or anyone who has not gone or struggles to go. Set a goal of going on a one week POG every year. If you can't do it, build to it. Get in a night here and a night there. Build up to the weekend getaway or the extended three night weekend vacation. Try to get 3-6 nights away every year.

The couple without a special needs kid should be doing a week a year. It is far easier for them in most cases. But you should be doing twice that! Because you need it twice as much. In many cases your family requires twice the work. In my own family I have a kid who needs half a parent, another who needs one parent, another who needs a parent and a half, and two who need two parents. And that is all the time. When my wife or I are at work, the parent on hand is BUSY!

You know your wife and family better than anyone. I should not tell you what to set for your goal, but just to set something. A week long outing is what you are building to. In good years past, Robin and I have done a one week POG twice a year plus a night here and there. Currently we are doing one week plus a night here and there. I hope to step that up however. If your work gives you two weeks off a year, give one to the family and one to your wife.

You are going this year, because you just threw down money on it. Set a goal to do it again. Build upon it, keep the ball rolling. Make it a tradition. I love it when my wife says, "I need a POG." All the creative juices start flowing and I dig deep to figure out how to make it happen. When there's a will there's a way. Set a POG goal and *make it happen!*

Rick and Robin's Pre-Planned POG

How did you do? Did you really do it? If not, grow a pair, go back and get 'er done. Here's what I did including costs and a few thoughts.

1. Formulate. Check. Right off the bat I totally deviated from what I said to do. This trip is not entirely about my wife. We just had a one night POG a couple months ago and I am sure she won't mind me being a little selfish on this trip.

2. Sitter. Got my mom for a two-nighter. It was easy to book her because it's for Robin's birthday. So she feels good about watching our kids plus it's a present to Robin. One of these days she will be too old to watch my kids. So I plan on taking advantage now and thanking God she is so good to us.

3. Money changes everything . The POG account is a little low. Cutting corners on some things and living it up on others.

4. Who is going? Ain't nobody going but the two of us. It is generally more difficult to plan with other couples and I am keeping this one simple.

5. How are you going to present this to your wife. My plan was to power point the POG like I was selling her a time-share. I've done this before and it works well.

I usually wait for a day that she has had enough and needs a good surprise. But I've been crazy busy lately and have not had time to put it on the computer. Then one night when we were together, I totally blew it and told her for no apparent reason other than I just couldn't hold back. Total rookie mistake! In my defense, I did need her input on a couple things to make sure she was cool with our plans and my selfishness.

6. When to go? Robin's birthday. Birthday POG!

7. Throw money at it. Check!

8. The basics. Here is the itinerary and costs.

Robin's Birthday

6:00AM: Sitter arrives and we leave shortly thereafter. No worries, my mom is a morning person. Drive to Long Beach. Cost of sitter, free!

7:00AM: Breakfast at Denny's because Robin eats free on her birthday! Maybe $15 for me and a tip.

8:00AM: Long Beach ferry departs for Two Harbors, Catalina Island. The ferry is free on your birthday! So Robin travels free and my fare is $75.

9:00AM: Arrive at Two Harbors. Leave our gear at the dock and run around town, explore, check into the dive shop, soak it all in. We have been to Avalon, the main town on Catalina a few times and love it. Two Harbors is something new.

12:00PM: our gear gets delivered to our campsite for $3. Campsite right on the water, $50. We set up camp and have lunch. The tentative plan for the day is rent a two-man kayak, paddle around, snorkel and spearfish. This is the selfish part. I like to camp more than Robin does. Our site is right on the water and because they deliver our gear, we can pack for camping comfort.

Also, I love to spearfish and don't get to do it much. Every now and then I really need to get out and kill something. Putting a shaft through a halibut's head and wrestling the creature to the surface while guts and blood gush out fulfills this urge. Hopefully, I will land something and take it to the restaurant for 'cook your catch,' or maybe Robin will be in the mood and we will cook it ourselves over the campfire.

There is hiking, and everything to rent from bikes to jet skies to stand-up paddleboards. Definitely not worried about things to do. Frankly, I'm really looking forward to being tired, stuffed, and lounging in our chairs at our campsite while the sun disappears. I'll get the fire going and we'll eat birthday s'mores while gazing over the glassy cove. Cost of rentals will depend on what we're feeling like. I'm guessing $75.

Day II

7:00AM: Breakfast at the restaurant. Cost $25.

8:00AM: Check in at dive shop for two tank boat dive. Cost $225. This should be the highlight of the trip.

12:00PM: our gear gets shipped back to the doc. $3. And we hang out on the sand, eat, whatever.

4:00PM: Ferry departs for Long Beach.

5:00PM: Check into the Long Beach Hilton Downtown. Cost 30,000 points. Once upon a time we did a POG to Puerto Vallarta. We stayed in a nice place for two days, decompressed, pampered Robin etc. Then we stuffed a backpack with only what we needed and jumped on a bus and headed north. We stayed cheap in a fishing/surf village, did all kinds of ocean and jungle adventures for a few days before heading back to PVR.

This was the best part of the trip. Tired, muddy, scratched up from our jungle excursions, and sweating like pigs, we walked into the lobby of the Marriott. I'm sure the staff thought we were going to ask for a handout. Imagine their surprise when we had a reservation. We went straight for the pool. You should have seen the cloud of muck when we dove in. Two nights at the Marriott after getting dirty was so nice.

And so in the spirit of you gotta earn it. We are getting dirty camping, diving and exhausting ourselves so as to earn a relaxing night at the Hilton. Pool, hot tub, chilling until checkout the next day. Food will be the only cost. Dinner $40.

Day III

Breakfast whenever? It's free at the hotel. Maybe bring it up and do breakfast in bed. Come home at noon. Cost of gas and ice cream on the way home, $20. Total duration, 3 days, 2 nights. Total cost $500. Keep in mind that we could easily do this trip for less than $100 if we wanted to pack our own food and not dive and rent kayaks. It would still be a successful POG in the books.

Post-POG

Yes I love technology
But, not as much as you, you see
But I still love technology
Always and Forever

      Kip Dynamite, Napoleon Dynamite

If you believe in an afterlife, what is it that you can take there? You are not taking your body. That is in the ground or scattered somewhere. You cannot take that truck sitting in your driveway or your prized collection of vinyl records. All that material stuff you are surrounded by stays right where it is. What you can take with you is what you learned, relationships, and your *experiences*. In short, every POG you take stays with you forever. Think for a moment of the value of a POG. Put it in monetary or whatever form you like. Even if you don't believe in life after death, was your last POG worth more than say your new computer? How about the new tile floor in your bathroom or couch in your living room? Your POG will still outlast everything you own.

These outings, although totally righteous, are a sacrifice. You spend money and lose time at work. You have created fond memories, but you still need to milk your POG for everything its worth. Pre-POG is filled with presentation and planning and anticipation. Post-POG you can squeeze sweetness out of for years to come. Here's how.

Remember all those pictures and videos you took on your trip? Sometimes it was inconvenient or you just didn't feel like taking out the camera. But a picture is worth a thousand words so you did it anyway. And now you are glad. Because the kids are kids and Mama Bear is out again. Life needs a little sunshine and those pictures can take her right back to that beach where she tried surfing for the first time. Timing is everything mind you, but pics and vids will absolutely take both of you back to that hotel, that sunset, that garden, that restaurant.

Technology is our friend, gentlemen. With it, we can organize all pictures and videos in no time. This is very important. You must make them *accessible*! Like many of you, I have cut the cable at the Daynes home. All computers including the flat screen on the wall have easy access to all Family and POG memories. Everyone knows where it is and how to access it in seconds. If your wife doesn't know it's there or how to get to it, you are defeating yourself. I have even written about some of our POGs so those journal entries are in the same files with the pictures. If you can put some memories on paper, all the better.

The most important post-POG project you do to make your wife happy is the POG Video. Within six months of any POG, no matter if it was a one-nighter or 10-dayer, you must create a video. Once again, technology is your friend. Chances are highly likely that you have software on your computer right now to create a decent and memorable video of your getaway. It doesn't have to be anything fancy or award winning. For some reason capturing the moments in high-def with music and perhaps some captions can make your POG look better than it actually was.

The problem is finding the time and actually doing it. That is why I have given you six months to put it together. <u>Your wife should not know about the video</u>. This is a present to be given to her six months after the main event. Also, if you haven't done it in six months, you won't do it at all. So after six months, find that teenager down the street or get it done professionally. If you can't find anyone, contact me and I'll give you my guy (www.keepittogetherman.org).

Memories

Life is a series of memories. Build upon them and enhance what you have already accomplished. Milk your vacations for everything they are worth. And they are worth everything. And 6 weeks, 6 months, 6 years later, when you have that quiet moment, however rare it might be, ask her, "Honey, what was the name of that restaurant we went to on our POG? Or what were you thinking when you jumped off that cliff, ate that green wormy dish, or scaled that wall? You will find that you are opening a window into that serenity and those beautiful moments you created.

I am not a poet, but when you are on a POG, you have a different mindset and are willing to do things you normally do not do. We have a small group of friends we like to cruise with. We call ourselves "The Doers." It's our little cruising club. Every time we line up a cruise, we extend the invitation out to a few more couples.

They almost always say no, because of the big three reasons we have already talked about.

Before dawn on our last full day at sea, I couldn't sleep. I left Robin in the cabin and went to a café where they serve the best doughnuts in international waters. I grabbed a doughnut and found a pencil and paper in the future cruise center. I scribbled the following poem on a Panama Canal cruise information form and presented it to the club that night over dinner.

The Doers

One hundred reasons

Not to go

Stay at home

Don't disrupt the flow

No time no money

Can't see through the smog

Lets take a chance!

It's time for a POG

Decompress, rejuvenate

Till your dipper is full

Rekindle the fire

And come back whole

So let the sitter take over

And clean up the manure

We're breaking free!

For we are the doers

The Rundown

1. Parents Only Getaway (POG) is huge!

2. Uncle Ed, the ironman of dating.

    A. Make dating a priority

3. The three great excuses

    A. No Time

    B. No Money

    C. No Sitter

    D. Take a chance and get it done

4. The King of Things. Respite

5. Alaska Brown Mama Bear. In order to leave the kid at home you need to overcome:

    A. Pride

    B. Shyness

    C. Mama Bear and fear of the sitter

6. POG Heaven is the gateway to the good life

7. POGing Made Easy. Book your POG now!

    A. Formulate

    B. Get a Sitter

    C. Money changes everything

    D. Who is going

    E. How are you going to present this to your wife

Sex

"Women need a reason to have sex. Men just need a place."

Billy Crystal

Ah yes, this is the chapter you have been waiting for. Most of you skipped ahead just to get a glimpse of the hidden secrets contained here. For this is where the secrets of a women's heart are unlocked. Where the mysteries of passion are unfolded and all your wildest dreams come true!

If you follow the steps in this chapter, you will be able to rekindle the physical intimacy you enjoyed prior to having kids. You thought you had it good your first year of marriage? Well, it's about to get even better! Your wife will want to have frequent, long lasting, passionate sex with you every night. Her sex drive will exceed your own, guaranteed!

But wait! There's more! If you act now and enroll in my 12 step "Till the Break of Dawn, Got It Going On" program, you'll receive a Michael Bolten CD absolutely free. You must call in the next 15 minutes to get the free CD. Are you ready? Operators are standing by. Just dial 1-800-Imfullofit.

I'd like to thank the gossip magazines at the grocery checkout line and the Cialis commercial I heard on the way home for inspiring the above plug for this chapter. There is no surefire sex remedy, but this is what we know for sure. For men, sex is the most powerful force in the universe! For women, sex is the most powerful force in the universe, until it's not, and then it's great and then it isn't and then oh, I just don't know... I'm not really feeling well.

Our sex drive is consistent and unchanged by natural or manmade disasters. Women's sex drive fluctuates by moods, seasons, the stock market, books, a whisper of air coming through a window, and the great unknown! Sex sells! And not just for men. Those magazines in the grocery checkout line are all designed for women. Sex was on the cover of all six of them. Women are ever changing and so constantly trying to figure themselves out. So they are curious about each magazine pitching this month's magic formula for sexy buns and an over-the-top climax.

You're in luck if your woman is giving any regard to those magazines or anything with sex in it, because at least it's on her mind at times. However, chances are the woman with a special kid has other things to think about. Thus your quest for sex is on.

Involuntary Pelvic Rest

"You ain't savin' the species tonight, or any other night." Ellie, Ice Age The Meltdown

Just prior to our first kid being born, we went on our last scheduled visit to Dr. Ob/Gyn. While there, the nurse looked at Robin and said, "After the baby is delivered, you need to be on pelvic rest for six weeks." The nurse then turned to me and asked, "Do you know what pelvic rest is?" My thought process went from John Travolta, to what we should avoid after an 8lbs baby traveled though my wife's birth canal. I was pretty sure I knew, but thought I'd give her the chance to explain anyway. She gave me a stern look and said, "No sex for six weeks. You got it? Can you do it? I'm serious, six weeks!" I felt like I had been scolded.

Two years later, in a different city, but on the same visit with baby number two on the way, I was asked the same question. "Do you know what pelvic rest is?" I did not forget my first experience but was curious to see if I'd get the same scolding. Her message was lighter, but with furrowed eyebrows for emphasis.

Two years later with baby number three (our last) on the way, and this time with the world's greatest Nurse Practitioner, the same question came. Robin knew where I was heading with it, so she cut me off and assured her that I knew. I then responded, "*Yep, I got it! No dancing for six weeks! He-he (MJ voice)*"

Five years later with baby number four (our last) 10 weeks away, Robin and I found ourselves in the recovery room after she had an emergency appendectomy. It was scary, lasted all night, and I was a bit of a wreck the next morning when the nurse asked me if I knew what six weeks of pelvic rest meant. Sex was the furthest thing from my mind as I was just glad the surgery was success-ful and my wife and unborn princess were fine. So I was annoyed by the question. After all, she knew Robin was pregnant with our fourth! It was probably the lack of sleep mixed with force of habit that I answered with a beaming, "Nope!"

What she said was, "Absolutely no sexual intercourse for six weeks." But the tone of her voice and non-verbal cues said, you along with all other men are nothing but a bunch of egotistical perverts! I was tempted to ask if there was a Mr. at home, but let it slide.

Going on pelvic rest is usually not that difficult because it coincides with a miracle like childbirth or some kind of injury or surgery. You can gear up for it and tell your mind and body that this is the way it's going to be. You understand completely your wife and the situ-ation and therefore you are supportive and content. The problems arise when pelvic rest does not coincide with any event and you don't understand anything about your wife and the situation and therefore you are non-supportive and malcontent.

Involuntary pelvic rest is written on the signpost above the door of your doghouse. This is not a happy place. You crawled through that doggie door far too many times and laid there in the fetal position far too long. Sometimes you deserve to be there. Sometimes you don't deserve to be there. And still other times you are there for no apparent reason at all! But there you are and there you sit. Just looking at the wall hangings, contemplating why you are there, how long you might be there, and what you can do to get out.

Move Over Fido! Dr. Laura is Man's Best Friend

Frankly, too many women treat their husbands as accessories instead of priorities.
Laura Schlessinger

I spend a lot of time in my car, so naturally, I surf the channels looking for songs and talk radio. When Doctor Laura was on the radio, I could not help but occasionally flip to her station. It is hard to pass up anyone giving free and uncensored advice on marriage while I am in the privacy of my own vehicle. Please don't tell anyone I listen to her! It could damage my rep.

Tens of thousands of women listen to and read Dr. Laura on a regular basis. Unfortunately, my wife is not among them. Here's why. Dr. Laura is black listed in liberal circles. My mother-in-law runs in those circles. Mother-in-law has far too much influence over my wife. Therefore, my wife doesn't listen to Dr. Laura.

A few years ago, Mama Bear was running rampant and I found myself in the doghouse so often, I hung curtains and matching lampshades. I found myself thinking, if I could just get Robin to listen to Dr. Laura, like my friends' wives, life would be so sweet. I had made the attempt a couple times before and knew that any further attempts would be in vain. Still, I held out hope that one day she might accidentally flip on the car radio and Dr. Laura might say something so profound it would draw Robin in.

The next day arrived and I was still decorating the doghouse. Sports talk shows became boring that afternoon, so I thought I'd check on Dr. Laura. Maybe she had a nugget that would help me out of my current living quarters? I flipped to her station and she wasn't there. I flipped to other stations and she wasn't there either. I called my underground network of men who listen to Dr. Laura and my worst fears were confirmed. She was gone. That night, after I installed recessed lighting in the doghouse, I penned the following letter to Dr. Laura.

Dear Dr. Laura,

Today, all men mourn. Our best friend, Dr. Laura, is no longer on the air. I am not sure why. Probably forced out by some political group that has nothing better to do than tear down all the good in the world. Listen you selfish whoremongers! Do you think Dr. Laura was too traditional? Too conservative? Did she offend you with teaching values? Did she belittle her guests? Was she rude? Well, how would you feel if a thousand women called you and said, "Hi Dr. Laura, thank you for taking my call. I am 23 years old and recently graduated from college. I've been living with my boy friend for four years now. He is unemployed, abusive, and I caught him in our bed with another woman. My mom keeps telling me to leave him now because he'll be in rehab for 90 days. But I just don't know. What should I do?" Do you think it is easy fielding that call 1000 times and giving the same advice over and over to women who just don't get it?

Dr. Laura, thank you for years of telling our wives that men are simple creatures. That we don't play mind games, nor do we read minds. That women have tremendous power over us and not to abuse that power. You have told them to be sweet and kind to us. You may not receive many phone calls and letters from men, but believe me, we are listening and appreciate what you do. Any woman who tells other women to put on a little something and take your husband to bed and make him feel like a man, and build him up. To be that damsel and let your man sweep you off your feet and be that hero. We won't admit it of course, but every man who has ever listened to you is cheering you on!

My Dr. Laura men's underground association, which will remain anonymous, has informed me that you have been a political target. All I can say is there is no socialist, libertarian, or a man in any political party, worldwide, who is happy about your absence. No one has helped more men get out of the doghouse than you. No one is more responsible for strengthening married couples than you. Your promotion of marriage and family values is unprecedented. Your straight talks that men only want to be happy and need only food and sex and not necessarily in that order, is the gospel truth!

We have lost our greatest ally! Fido has taken a back seat, and you, Dr. Laura, are man's best friend.

Sincerely,

Rick Daynes

Mama Bear Ain't Having Sex With Nobody

Yeh, so…um, I never sent the letter. I'm not a letter guy. I don't suppose there are many among us. We don't write letters, and if we do, we don't send them. We don't talk to each other, rarely ask for directions or read the directions. It's a wonder we figure anything out. And speaking of figuring things out, why is the sex chapter under the "Happy Wife Happy Life" section? Answer: because if your wife isn't happy, she isn't having sex.

If she is not happy, there is a good chance Mama Bear is on the prowl. And Mama Bear ain't having sex with nobody. So, without further ado, direct from the men's underground of Dr. Laura listeners, here is how you turn it all around and *make all your wildest dreams come true (Pedro voice, Napoleon Dynamite)*. A few nuggets anyway.

1. First thing you have to do is have empathy. Put yourself in your wife's shoes. She is busy. She is tired and battling every day. Everyone in your household relies on her and wants things from her including you. Think about her day today. How many poopy diapers has she changed? How many mouths did she feed? How many fires did she put out and how many did she create? How is she faring in the everyday unpredictable nature of raising a special kid? Is she stressing over your child's progress or lack thereof? Is she getting along with the teacher, therapists, family members and friends, or is she dealing with a hundred other variables in her everyday life? Think for a moment about the day-to-day monotony of it all. Grinding it out each and every day and then you show up without any regard for what

she's been through, and you want to rough house. Know where she is coming from and show empathy, kindness, and support.

2. Focus on the basic points in the previous chapters. It is already spelled out for you! All talk show hosts have their own style. The more you listen to them, the more you become accustomed to their vernacular and buzz words. Sometimes you get to know them so well, you know what they are going to say when callers ask for advice or challenge them. Well, there is one word that is not thrown around guy circles. We just never say the word. It's uncomfortable and awkward for a lot of us and certainly me, but not to Dr. Laura. She throws it around like a Frisbee. And that word is…ugh…I just cannot say it!

   I know! It's even hard to write. Okay… The word is… orgasm. There, I said it! It has got to be Dr. Laura's favorite all-time word. She talks about it. She encourages it. Guys don't use that word because we have no problem with it. If we have sex, we're having an orgasm. But that is not the case with women, and Dr. Laura chucks it around like a catcher throwing the ball around the horn after a strikeout. Except she doesn't need the bases clear. She throws that ball around any time, with men on base or not. She doesn't even need a strikeout. She is throwing that ball around the horn, because she wants women to have them and experience it all the time.

You would do well to adopt that attitude. I was recently out with a group of business associates that I have known for a long time. After everyone had some drinks, the topic went to sex. Funny how that happens. It didn't take long before one woman let all of us know that sex is overrated.

Does your wife think sex is overrated? Because if she does, that's on you. If your wife is not climaxing, or at least close to it, that is a reflection of you. A women's body is complex. Many woman have difficulty achieving an orgasm. If they don't get there, make sure it is not from a lack of trying. Sex is fun for you, sure. But is it fun for her? How often will she have sex if she is not having orgasms?

If you want your wife to have sex with you, then you better do everything you can to make sure she is having a good experience. Take care of her first! Make sex about her, and sometimes, if you are lucky, she will make it about you. Resist the urge to be selfish in bed. If she won't let you experiment and figure things out, then slowly break down those walls and try something new until it works. *"Let me ask you a question. This new move. Is there a knuckle involved in any way?" George Costanza, Seinfeld*

I will never forget taking a health course in College. This was at a community college in Southern California with a wide variety of ethnicities and ages. The class was about 50/50 men to women. Our teacher gave us a quiz on sex before we entered the sex chapter, just to see what we thought. He asked the question: True or false: Sex is something a man does to a woman? The results shocked me. Would you believe that 35% of the class answered true!

I could not believe anyone could possibly think that. I wanted to stamp "idiot" on the forehead of every person in that 35%. No names were given though, only the final tally. If you think sex is something a man does to a woman, you definitely need some work.

Here Comes the Bride

Oh! and one last nugget. Marriage is about giving yourself to one another. Think about your wedding day and the vows the two of you made. You gave yourselves to each other in front of witnesses. Following the party you consummated your marriage through sex. Hopefully, you did that without witnesses. But you should know that some time ago there were cultures that would have a witness or two on site for the consummation.

Can you imagine that? Okay, groom and bride, you each have to choose one person to witness the consummation. Both families, the town, everyone needs verification that this marriage agreement is complete just in case one of you decides to run back to your family. So let's see, witnessing for the bride we have her mother. And for the groom, Uncle Si, so the mother of the bride and Uncle Si take ring side seats for the evening's main event. Uncle Si decides to stand up nearly spilling his iced tea and says, "*Hey, look here. You're going about this all wrong. Hey, when it comes to sex, I've got more experience in my pinky finger than you'll ever have, Jack (Uncle Si voice Duck Dynasty)!*"

There may be something you do in your daily life that reminds you of who you are or who you want to be. Perhaps you or your work has a Mission statement. Goals do the same thing. You have certain guidelines or rules you follow to remind and keep yourself or your marriage in line. Your wife wears a wedding ring. You wear yours too. Or maybe sometimes you do or maybe you don't. You prefer to consummate your marriage regularly, a reminder that you have given yourselves to each other. The Mrs. is on board from day one until day......

Let's go back to day one. Think about your wedding day. What was that all about? Who planned it? Who spent the money? Who was it most important to? Who chose the venue, the colors, the meal? Who cared about all the arrangements? Planning the wedding is a good exercise for future husbands because it gets them in the habit of agreeing with everything the bride wants. "Yes dear."

Maybe you really had input in your wedding. But the wedding itself, with all the trimmings was all about your wife. Who walks down the isle last? Who do they stand up for? Who is the dominant figure? Do you think the audience was whispering to themselves, "I can't wait to see the groom and the tuxedo he's wearing?" NO! Of course not! They cannot wait to see the bride! They gasp when they see her, and they all gawk and make a fuss over how beautiful she is and her wedding dress is just perfect.

Think of how she feels on that pedestal. Everyone is there to see her. She is the focal point. This woman gave herself to you. But this is her day! You are surrounded by people all day long. Eventually, you whisk her away from the crowds. You have stolen her away. She is yours now and you are hers. It is the beginning of a new life. Then you engage in the last thing that is part of the marriage ceremony (tradition). You consummate or complete the marriage.

Look at her now. Is she as happy as she was that day? Probably not, that was her wedding day. Well, is she generally happy or sad? If you could, would you give her that day again? That day when she was perfect, when she was the bride? How many problems would be eliminated if you could just rekindle a part of that day? She would certainly be happier. There would be no need for a chapter on sex.

So what is stopping you? She deserves at the very least a sincere effort from you on a regular basis. Put her on a pedestal. Make her feel like she is the focal point, the center of attention, the bride you married. I am not saying throw her in front of a crowd and sing her a song, unless she loves it that way. Be creative and resourceful. If you're not used to doing special things for your wife you may have to dig deep. Make her feel special. She should be more special to you now than she was then. Remind her of the bride she is and perhaps she will be reminded of the groom you are.

Armageddon

She's up all night to the sun
I'm up all night to get some
She's up all night for good fun
I'm up all night to get lucky

Daft Punk, Get Lucky

I don't like to be negative and especially not end a chapter or section on a negative note. But this needs to be said. You could be up all night to get some. You could be up all night to get lucky. You could be a great guy who loves his wife unconditionally, who treats

212

her like a queen day in and day out. You could have had all the stars align, the tide on the rise, the clock in your favor, and you won the lottery earlier that day. The heavens have opened and all signs are pointing to your bed. Unfortunately your wife sensed a tad bit of anxiety in your movement and all adult privileges for the night have been suspended.

You cannot overstate the power of sex or lack thereof. Historically, it has been the source behind monumental decisions. Most of which were bad. Murders, revolutions, and wars have been spurred and fueled by sex. Doom and gloom have set upon you as everything will never line up like that again. Your moment passed in defeat, and for you, this is the end of the world.

Nobody knows but you, your wife, your situation, your pain. Forget sex, to have a little kindness would be glorious. A little understanding, nirvana. But no. Maybe your wife is just cruel. Or maybe you are the pig. It could be both. Sometimes there is nothing you can do. You pin your hopes on her changing. She might be thinking the same thing. You have been put on extended pelvic rest for no apparent reason. You are humbled and it hurts.

You have tried everything from dates to prayer and still, no change. But women change all the time. Today it's a famine but tomorrow could be feast. It may be a good marriage gone bad, or a bad marriage gone worse. Or you could be totally overreacting! Counseling might work, and it might not. It is hard to decide what to do when things get rocky, both in marriage and in bed. The two are synonymous for you, but not for her.

Answers are hard to come by and you take a long look within. What do you need to change about yourself? What has to change about your marriage? Only you can decide. No one knows but you. But keep this in mind when diving into the soul of a wounded man. Keep your emotions in check as much as possible. Never ever make decisions in the heat of an argument or late at night. Emotions always run higher at night. Don't go to war if all you need is to ride out the storm.

Most likely this is one of the many times in your life when you need to buck up and endure. You get stronger and stronger with each trial. The harder the trial, the stronger you become. Things have a way of working themselves out. It has worked out for you a thousand times and will another ten thousand. Change will come in some form and life will be sweet again. Don't throw away something that is rotten at the moment. It could be far sweeter later. There is a reason you took that vow in the first place. Honor it. Give it everything you have, even if all you have left is humility.

The Run Down

1. For men, sex is the most powerful force in the universe! For women, sex is the most powerful force in the universe, until it's not, and then it's great and then it isn't and then oh, I just don't know... I'm not really feeling well.

2. Involuntary Pelvic Rest. Any way you slice it, it sucks.

3. Move Over Fido! Dr. Laura is Man's Best Friend.

   A. An educated, thoughtful woman on the radio pleading our case with women. Invaluable.

   B. Now she is gone and we have lost our greatest ally in our battle to educate our wives of our simple needs.

4. Mama Bear Ain't Having Sex With Nobody. If there is any hope, you must soften Mama Bear.

   A. Show empathy.

   B. Focus on the points we have already discussed in Happy Wife Happy Life.

   C. Give her a good experience under, between, or on top of the sheets. Or possibly in another room, or time of day, or...just figure it out!

5. Here Comes the Bride. Make her your bride again and again.

6. Armageddon.

   A. If you have done all you can do and love is absent. It is not the end of the world.

   B. Do not make any decisions when emotional.

   C. Be strong! Make correct decisions. Ride out the storm. You will be a better man for it.

Part IV

The Club

The Club

I would like to formally welcome you to The Club. The Club has no formal or informal meetings. It has no boundaries, handshakes, or rituals. It is not affected by politics, race, gender, education, or other organizations. We rarely speak of it, and most members do not even know they are a part of it, though it definitely exists.

The club has a power that cannot be suppressed. Its influence is vast with a worldwide membership. It is made up of people, like yourself, who have something special. It is hard to define what it is, but let's take a stab at it.

If you look at a handicapped child and think how beautiful that kid is, you're in the club! If you know a couple, who is going into their first IEP meeting, and you offer to help them, you're in! If you are perceptive enough to see that your nephew needs to feel special, and you make it happen, you, my friend are way in! If you wish that woman would keep her baby quiet on the plane, you're out!

Carson and Jack are playing at recess. The two have been in the same class and soccer team for a few years and are friends. Carson takes Jack's ball. Jack tackles Carson to get his ball back. Jack, who has special needs, is sent to the principal's office and suffers the consequences. Carson's mom is upset, emotional, and wants further action. Carson's mom just doesn't get it. She's out.

Devon is out of town on Valentine's Day. Devon's neighbor, Larry, calls Devon to ask if he arranged anything for his wife. Devon, who completely forgot about Valentine's Day, admits he's got nothing. Larry then says to Devon, "I got your back. I'm making a u-turn to the flower shop now and will have something at her door within the hour." Larry get's it! He's in.

Most of the members share a special bond, and that is our children. You will find numerous websites for different organizations for kids with various special needs all over the world. The Club encompasses all of them. Your local Down Syndrome association, Autism support group, Cerebral Palsy organization are all subgroups of The Club. Eventually, you will notice more special needs kids than ever. You just know who they are and where they are, even if they look completely normal.

You will look at their parents and have instant compassion and empathy for the struggles they have been through and for what lies ahead. And yet at the same time you will get this warm fuzzy feeling inside and think that couple hit the jack-pot! To the outside world, that does not make any sense. Those are two emotions at opposite ends of the spectrum. How can a challenging life of caring for a handicap person equate to hitting the jack-pot? It just does. And members of The Club get it. If you don't get it now, don't worry, you will.

Initiation

YOU DO NOT NEED TO HAVE A KID WITH SPECIAL NEEDS NOR HAVE A RELATIVE OR CONNECTION WITH ANY PERSON WITH SPECIAL NEEDS IN ORDER TO GAIN ENTRANCE INTO THE CLUB. Some people are just in. It is the way they are.

We answered a Craigslist add for a lady who wanted to work with Autistic kids. Her two children had flown the coup and she simply wanted to give back and make a difference. She came over to our home once or twice a week for months, just to play and work with our Tyler. No need to tell you that lady is not only in The Club, she's a Chapter President.

You, my friend, are in The Club by virtue of having a special child. That kid of yours will be responsible for your initiation. At times he or she will designate your wife or someone else to send a dose of initiation your way. You must understand that this is not a onetime initiation. Membership requires an ongoing process with

219

dues to pay. Dues may come up weekly or even daily for a time. They could taper off to monthly, and then again, they might not. It all depends. If you want to be a member of the club, and believe me, you do, you will go through these initiations just to keep your membership current and in good standing.

Sometimes you will love to pay your dues! You hit it head on and do it with a smile. Still, there will be many times when paying your dues will feel like it's not worth it. Coach Kinsfather may show up and say, "Boy, I aint gona lie to you. Tomorrow, you are going to get your butt kicked." You'll feel like you just can't take it anymore. After all, there is a good chance you did not sign up for this! And then you will be reminded in a thousand different ways, that there is nothing as valuable as membership in The Club. Plus, these initiations are vital in developing your life, skills, and super powers.

Super Powers

"It's not who I am underneath, but what I do that defines me."
Bruce Wayne, Batman Begins

Much has been said about women and what they are expected to be. Dress like an actress, be as shapely as a Barbie doll. Women trying to live up to images on magazine stands. The pressures and problems associated with women's psychology and self-esteem are boundless.

Well, how about us? What about the modern man? Do we glorify the sensational? *Heck yes we do (Napoleon Dynamite voice)*. Like moms, dads are taking on more and more responsibilities. We are busy! Busy keeping it all together man.

I just read another Dan Brown novel. The characters I read about in fictional books can save the world, but they cannot do what you and I do every day. Harvard professor and renowned symbologist Robert Langdon can't touch you. He can only dream about doing what you do! Wouldn't you love to do a life swap with that guy? Rick Daynes is now the Harvard professor. I think I will hang loose around campus before my afternoon class. Maybe catch up with some people after work and do a little research. Yeah, I will probably Google whatever it is I am working on.

 Robert Langdon woke at 2:00AM to the shrieking sounds of a crying baby. In his terry cloth robe he staggered to the child's room to assess the situation. The facial expression of the baby was foreign to the professor. It was not until he used his nose that he was able to diagnose the problem. The Pungent odor clearly said this was a messy diaper that needed immediate attention.

The baby was uncooperative with the diaper change, arching his back and turning over every time an attempt was made to remove the diaper. Professor Langdon eventually transferred the subject from the changing table to the floor and had to pin the kid down with his leg while he somewhat successfully wiped the poop off the youngster. The situation got more sticky when the child was able to free a leg and wildly kick it around causing the mess to spread all over the child, the floor, and Langdon.

The situation now moved to the bathroom where a hose down of Langdon and the screaming child proved successful. He put the kid in bed with his mother while Langdon turned his attention to the poop on the floor and walls and cracks and how the heck did it get over there! Upon completion, Langdon discovered the child wide awake in his bed. He spent the next 60 minutes rocking and attempting to put the child down. Eventually, the kid won the battle and Robert slept the rest of the night in the rocking chair with the baby.

Langdon missed his 5:00AM swim because he was exhausted. He did eventually make it out of the house to go to work. However, he left with snot on the shoulder of his Harris tweed jacket and a ketchup stain on the front crotch section of his pants. His four year old boy had ketchup on his face as he embraced the tall Langdon, transferring ketchup to his pants and racking his balls simultaneously. Running to his car because his daughter wanted to go with him, he stepped on a land mine on the front lawn. The dog who left the present was undoubtedly his neighbor's. The professor quickly stowed his loafers in his trunk, then drove away in his socks as fast as possible. Minutes later he kicked the camera man out of his car, called the producer of Life Swap, and explained that he would not participate anymore.

How long would Jack Reacher, Mitch Rapp, or James Bond last in your shoes? A day? Maybe? They cannot do what you do! Shoot, those guys cannot even maintain a relationship. In the fictional world, they are fun to read. In reality, you are kicking their trash every day of the week! You have powers! Super dad powers. The Club powers.

Every time you pay your dues, you increase your powers. The more you use your powers, the stronger you get. You have the power to diffuse an angry child, melt Mama Bear into sweetness, and turn a bad IEP into a great one. You perceive thoughts, you know what is going to happen next, and you know who is on your side simply by using your powers. Call it Intuition, charity, resourcefulness. You will have it if you don't already. All you have to do is let it in, and rock it.

The Friendly Neighborhood Stalker

"You must feel the force around you." Master Yoda, Star Wars

Shortly after our Eli was born, I noticed I was seeing a lot more special needs kids. In particular, kids with Down Syndrome or some kind of chromosome issue. I would pass a kid who has Down Syndrome on the street and five minutes later sit down in a restaurant and a another kid with Down Syndrome would come sit next to me. I figured there were always special needs kids around me, I just never noticed.

I began talking to parents and grandparents who had these special kids, and started having even more encounters. Once this kid in a wheelchair came by with the biggest smile you ever saw just staring right at me. Ten minutes later I was at a stop sign while a special needs class crossed right in front of me. I waved to a few of them and they loved it. Ten minutes later I went into a fast food place and sure enough here is this totally cool special needs kid busing my table. Sometimes I have so many encounters; I look around for cameras because I swear someone is playing a joke on me.

A year after Eli was born I was in the waiting area getting ready to board a plane after a week of work in another city. I saw this good looking young man who had Down Syndrome with his parents waiting to board the same plane. I was tempted to talk to them, but thought I would leave them alone. I am one of those guys who likes to board last. I know, not too many of us. But I am just fine not sitting on the plane forever. In any case, I was boarding last and you know what was going through my mind? I am thinking this flight is completely full, but I can almost guarantee that young man with Down Syndrome will be in the seat next to me. I just know it!

I got on the plane and looked back to a completely full plane. Three fourths of the way down the isle I saw one empty seat. My seat. As I approached my seat, I noticed the guy with Down Syndrome was not in the seat next to me. He was in the seat in front of me. I was actually a little disappointed, until I sat down and realized the guy in the seat next to me was his dad.

I told him I was in The Club, and that I just knew I would be sitting next to his boy on this plane. I told him that special needs people, along with their families, were stalking me. And yet, I loved it. He reminded me that I was last to sit down, so therefore I was no longer being stalked, but now the stalker.

For the next two hours he told me everything I needed to know about raising a child who has Down Syndrome. Ever wish your flight time was longer? Well, I could have flown all day with this family. We emailed each other a week later. Two weeks after that, he sent me a gold medal his son won in the Special Olympics! But wait, there's more! He also sent me a complete copy of his son's Special Needs Trust!

One of your powers will be an instant friendship and love to all special kids and their families. You will gravitate to them, and they to you. We call this your Special Needs Radar or SNR. No one knows quite how this happens. It can only be explained as part of your super powers. You know when you bought that car and now that you're driving it around, you notice that same car is everywhere. It is kind of like that, but to the 10th power, plus your warm fuzzy meter goes crazy every time you have a special needs encounter.

When that meeting happens, please be aware of Mama Bear. She doesn't know you! You pay attention to her special kid. You begin a conversation, and Mama Bear jumps in wondering who the heck you are. Just let her know you are in The Club, and it's all good.

Last week, I took my boys to Petco Park to watch a Padre game. Petco Park is a great ball park if you have kids who can't sit still to watch a game. I have two to four kids in that category depending on their mood, sleep, food, weather, and the tide. In straight away center field they have a giant sand box. Beyond that is the Park in the Park, which is essentially a large grass hill and field about the size of a football field. Beyond that is a playing area for kids with slides and bars and all that. To the side of the hill is a miniature baseball field where Padre employees pitch wiffle balls to kids.

I set up a blanket on the top of the hill so I can watch my kids play at the miniature field or wherever they might roam. We arrived an hour and a half early to the game, so my boys could watch batting practice. I am the only one on the hill. In fact, I am the only one set up in the entire park in the park. I am just lying out on my blanket taking it all in. Sure enough along comes this guy pushing a stroller and he plops down right next to me. It's like being the only one in a movie theater and you are sitting on the top corner of the stadium, and someone comes and sits down right next to you.

My SNR (Special Needs Radar) is pinging loudly between my ears. I say hi, then notice the stroller is not a typical baby stroller. The stroller was facing away from me, so I got up and walked around the dad and stroller to get a look of what is inside. The dad doesn't give the slightest hint that this is awkward. A strange man who was lying on a blanket gets up and walks around to see what is inside. It happens to him all the time! Members of the Club having their SNR go off and they feel compelled to check out what treasure is in the stroller. Sure enough, it is a beautiful eight year old girl who has Down Syndrome.

I am new to the world of Down Syndrome, but this sweet girl could not walk or talk and probably functions at a 8-10 month old level, but what an absolute angel! Again, I am new at this. People probably look at my two year old who has Down Syndrome and say he's low functioning. But to me, he is a rock star! I met her parents, grandparents, and two younger siblings. Yes, that's right. They have this sweet sweet jewel who requires a lot of care, and yet they have two adorable kids after her. It gets better. He is a teacher and his wife looks like she belongs on the cover of a magazine. No doubt this dad graduated suma cum laude at The Club Academy, as the force is strong with this one.

Ranking

"With great power comes great responsibility." Uncle Ben, Spiderman

If you see a woman in a store who is struggling with a kid or two or five, and you think she should do a better job keeping her kids quiet, or make them behave, you are not in the Club. If you have empathy for her, you are in the Club. If you establish eye contact and smile at them, you are a Tender Foot in The Club. If you offer her help, you are Second Class. If she is reluctant to accept your help, but you manage to help anyway and play with her kids and put a smile on everyone's face, you are First Class!

The Club does have a ranking system. It is self-ranked and regulated. After all, who knows where your heart is? Who knows what service you provide for your family, for your neighbor, for a complete stranger? Only you know the power of the force within you. Well you and Master Yoda, but he is not around much. It grows and fluctuates with every victory and defeat you have.

The service you render, the attention to your family and love you give is empowering and moves you up through the ranks. Consequently, withholding your talents, failing to date your wife, and being absent from your child's IEP will send you sliding. There are no outside forces that decide your rank. Rather it is your reaction to outside forces and problematic situations which determine where you stand and who you are. Let me give you three great examples. All of whom just happen to be in the same story.

Eli

Six and a half weeks before Robin was due to deliver Eli, our last child who has Down Syndrome, I took a flight to San Francisco to work for the week. I got there at night and went to sleep about 11:00PM. An hour and a half later at 12:30AM my cell rang. Robin's water had broken, and Eli was coming into this world six weeks premature. Rather than wait for a morning flight, I jumped in my car and took off for home, an eight hour drive minimum. While speeding away, I orchestrated the event. I woke up my mom and told her she was to get to my home and take care of my kids. I woke up Robin's sister and told her she needed to get to the hospital and take my spot. I spoke to the hospital and let them know a high risk pregnancy lady was driving herself in and they'd better be ready. I talked to Robin several times of course, talking her through this.

Robin delivered all our kids pretty fast to Millennium Falcon light speed. So I was sure I would miss the birth. However, Eli had other ideas and six hours after she called me, I was there without a single speeding ticket. We welcomed Eli a few hours later and life in the Neonatal Intensive Care Unit (NICU) for a premature baby with Down Syndrome and associated problems began.

That was a crazy day, and the following days did not let up. Eventually Robin was discharged, but she rarely left the hospital. She was in hyper-active-mama- bear mode. She was going to feed her baby. She was going to change diapers. She was going to tend to her baby's needs. If you were Eli's nurse while he was in the NICU, your job was cake! I had our mini van detailed and took out all the seats. The kids and I decorated the interior with family pictures and made mommy a new bedroom where she could rest at the hospital. Robin started coming home after the 11:00PM feeding and going back for the 6:00AM feed. I was in hyper-active-full-support-of-mama-bear-mode. When you see your infant hooked up to all kinds of wires and tubes and monitors, ugh, your heart just melts.

I was a zombie taking care of our four kids at home, plus everything that goes along with mom duties, plus my work. Enter example number one, Lisa. Lisa came to us one day and said, "Anything you need, just call." We currently have three boys in baseball. That's two games a week per kid plus practices. Plus one of them needs me there in case of a melt down, leaving the field, you know, the usual. Well, Lisa persisted, because she has super natural powers and knew I was drowning. She became my go-to person when I needed someone to pick up a kid from baseball or whatever.

One day Super Lisa sent me an email with two attachments. Attachment number one is a list of people who will be bringing our family dinner every night. Attachment number two is a list of people who will watch Summer, our three-year old, for a few hours every day so I can work. I was shocked! I went down the schedule. There were names from neighbors, friends, church folks, and baseball families. Apparently Super Lisa was doing more than picking up our kids from baseball.

About two weeks after Eli was born, things went from crazy to ludicrous. Our good friends who were so good to take Summer for an afternoon, sent her back to us with the flu. Can you imagine how they must have felt? Yeesh. I called Robin and told her not to come home. If she did, for sure she was not going back into the NICU. I delivered fresh clothes and uncontaminated supplies to her.

We hunkered down and let that stomach virus run it's course with Summer and then with Tyler, and then with Jefferson, and then me. YES! Freaken awesome! Love it! Oh man, it was brutal. Enter Phyllis, example number two. She messages me one day and tells me she has too many credits with her cleaning service. So she is going to send them to my place. First of all, I don't believe her. Second, no way am I going to accept that. So I turn her down. However, Phyllis has super-human powers and she knows I am running on fumes and will break down any day. So she persists.

I am not used to accepting services from others. But with your newborn baby, with Down Syndrome, who has a hole in his heart, not sure if he has any hearing, bad eye sight and who knows what else. They seem to be testing for new defects every other day. My wife was living at the hospital and I was cleaning up barf and taking care of sick kids while my business was failing and little money was coming in. Life has a way of humbling you. And I was certainly humbled. So while I'm hugging the throne myself, I consented to the cleaning crew coming over.

A week later, the virus was out of our home and out of our lives. It got everyone but our seven-year-old, Jeremiah. What a huge boost it was to have professional cleaners come in and clean the house. Eli was doing better at the hospital and things were looking up for the Daynes family! That is until the morning's doctor visit, and the doctor said, "Hey Eli is looking good, he's right on track to go home in three more weeks." Ugh. Three more weeks! What a depressing moment that was. We wanted so badly for that kid to come home! For his mom to come home! To get going on life! What a downer.

That is until a different doctor came by a few hours later and said, "Hey Eli is looking good, how would you like to take him home today? Oh Doctor (Jerry Coleman voice)!!!! I cannot tell you how excited we were to hear those words. To finally bring that baby home. If you are keeping score at home. The morning doctor...not in The Club. Afternoon doctor...definitely in The Club! We were over-joyed. Upon hearing the news, our Jeremiah was so excited he threw up.

Turns out he didn't escape the bug. He just let it fester for a week before letting it manifest. Maybe he didn't want to join the barf fest of the prior week? I don't know, he's always been a little different. Oh, why can't we schedule the flu? I called Robin to tell her

228

the bad news. "We cannot bring that baby home yet, Jeremiah just started vomiting." The party was over. Still, in my head I was working on a plan. There had to be a way.

I was encouraged, because a few days prior to this we had scheduled a second disinfecting of our house. Supposedly, Phyllis had more extra credits than she thought. Yeah right. But they were on their way over and I could not believe this could be a coincidence. Cleaning crew just happens to be coming over hours before our baby is coming home? That cannot be a coincidence. I thought, if I could just get rid of Jeremiah, the cleaning crew could clean and we could bring that baby home. I thought about taking him to a hotel, but I was needed to get kids places. I thought about people and family. I finally got the nerve to call my mom and explain the situation.

You'll recall from the POG chapter that my mom rocks! She is awesome and does so much for us. All her kids and grandkids and countless others love her. She has a resumé of service and giving and understanding longer than the eye can see. But she was not in the Club. At least, at this point she was not in the Club. Well, how can that be? How can she be so sweet and not in the Club? Hey, just because you're a rockin' grandma doesn't mean you get it. The special needs world is a different animal. It is hard to get it. And that's okay.

My mom declined to take my sick kid. Hey, how many people would? She doesn't want to get sick. In her mind, she's thinking, that baby is in a good place in the hospital. Robin is fine. Go a few more days and let Jeremiah get rid of this sickness and then bring that baby home. No big deal.

I, however, was crushed. I should not have been crushed because I expected her response. But after several weeks of grinding it out every day, getting my butt kicked by the flu, work, kids, and life, I was spent. My wife wanted badly to come home. I wanted her home so badly I was willing to do anything. And to have our new baby home, without a feeding tube and oxygen in his nose and wires and needles stuck to his feet and arms, was too overwhelming to think about. I don't expect everyone to understand, but to me, getting my family home under our roof represented the end of a sore battle and the beginning of a new chapter.

Enter example number 3, Alice. After I got off the phone with my mom, Alice's special needs radar was screaming! She called me minutes later and asked what was going on. I told her the situation and that everything was cool.

Alice: How about I come over and get Jeremiah and take him to my house for a few days.

Rick: That's very thoughtful Alice, but all is good. We'll just have Robin and Eli stay at the hospital a few more days until Jeremiah gets healthy.

Alice: Are you sure? Really, I could come over right now. You can get your house cleaned up and go get them.

Rick: Alice, he is barfing every 20 minutes. He is highly contagious. You don't want to bring that into your home. Your family will get sick. Violently sick! Really, we're good. It'll be fine.

Alice: Don't worry about us. We won't get sick. I'm coming over.

Rick: Wait. Uh…. Really? No, Alice, thanks so much, but we cannot ask you to do that..

The conversation continued with that theme until Jeremiah eventually ended up at Alice's house kneeling over her toilet and passing out on her bathroom floor. I spent the next couple hours with Phyllis's cleaning crew sanitizing every inch of the house. I then went to the hospital and brought Eli and Robin home. You know that feeling when you bring a newborn home? With Eli, the feeling was off the chart. My heart pounded, yet I was calm and there was peacefulness in our home that was so incredibly sweet. It's hard to describe. I guess I would say it was magic.

Here's what you should know about the three examples. I am Facebook friends with one of them. None of them is a part of our lives really. Between Robin and me, we have hundreds of friends and neighbors we know far better than these three. We have hundreds of friends and family members with whom we feel closer. So why these three? Why didn't a family member or close friend step up? Certainly, many of them knew we were struggling. There were those who gave help and offered help, but we turned them away for the most part. We certainly did not ask for any help, although we should have. Yet the most unlikely people took it upon themselves to get involved in our drama. Why?

It's all about the Club. Lisa has one grandchild with Down Syndrome and another who is about 10 years old and has been in a wheelchair his whole life. I am not sure what he has exactly, but I know there are multiple issues. Despite having a full time job, she manages to fly to Canada on a regular basis to watch these kids, plus some, so her daughter can take a POG. Oh, and she adores these kids!

Phyllis has three young very active children. All three of them are on the spectrum. Alice has three children. The youngest is in high school. All three have IEP's. Alice also has a brother with Down Syndrome. All three women have, sensed our grief, befriended us, rendered us service we badly needed, and given us part of themselves. Come on man! Who is going to take a vomiting seven year old into their home? Who does that? I don't! Heck no! No way am I bringing a bug into my house. But super heroes do super things.

Perhaps one day I will advance my rank in The Club to that of these three heroes. I might even take a sick kid into my house. Probably won't happen until I get rid of a couple kids of my own. Nevertheless, it could happen. I did not used to think this, but it is within me. The challenges of Club membership have serious rewards. With every due you pay, rewards pour in. Some are as subtle as finding joy in your daughter's smile. While others are as obvious as people lining up meals, cleaning your home, and taking your sick boy under their roof so you can bring home a new baby.

It is within you also. You might have to let go of yourself, your current life. Sacrifices are inevitable. The more you give in and embrace life with a special kid, the more you will enjoy. You won't understand it until you get there, but things will happen to you. It won't be like Spiderman. You won't get bit by an insect and wake up the next morning shooting webs out of your wrist. That story is fictitious anyway. But yours is not. Your life is real. Your story is real.

Coach V

When I was a kid, I loved basketball. I loved to play it, watch it, and follow it in both college and pros. Over the years, my love for basketball has tapered off, but I'm still excited when March Madness rolls around. For me and perhaps for you, the NCAA's (National Collegiate Athletic Association) tournament every March is one of the greatest sporting events of the year. You never know who is going to get knocked out early and who is going to emerge out of nowhere. I guess I love the drama and the stories associated with this tournament. There is nothing like a good sports story, and there is no tournament like this.

I was in elementary school when I watched the greatest Cinderella story in the history of the tournament. North Carolina State had no business even being in the tournament. They had 10 losses that year and had to win their conference tournament to make it in. Well, when you are playing in the ACC (Atlantic Coast Conference) and you've got to take on teams like North Carolina, the defending National Campion with Michael Jordan, and Virginia with one of the games most dominating centers in Ralf Sampson, this is a daunting task at best. But they managed to do it and get into the tourney.

They had no super star player, and every game was an unbelievable come from behind victory in the closing seconds. I believe they won 7 of their last 9 games after trailing with a minute left in the game. Being down by six with two minutes to go seemed to be the theme to their run. What makes it down right ridiculous is that there was no three-point line, nor a shot clock yet in college basketball. So these come from behind victories are more mind boggling now if you think about it. I remember thinking they just got lucky every game. Until they got lucky too many times for anyone to think this wasn't something special.

They matched up in the finals against one of the greatest college teams ever assembled. Clyde Drexler, Hakeem Olajuwon and the rest of Houston's Phi Slama Jama were going to crush North Carolina State and everyone knew it. Well, everyone except for the kids sitting on NC State's bench, and possibly a few of their fans.

The Cinderella story concluded with a long unintentional alley-oop dunk at the buzzer sending onlookers into mind numbing shock and North Carolina State into sports history. To this day, the image of that final basket followed by an Italian guy running all over the court is familiar to even the most casual sports fans.

Ten years later, ESPN hosted its first ESPY awards. Now a young adult, I watched as that same Italian guy running around the court years earlier, stepped feebly to the podium with the aid of Dick Vital. I did not know much about Coach Jim Valvano back then. I knew he was the coach of that unbelievable team and had heard he was a charming and charismatic guy. I knew that he had terminal cancer and that he was approaching death. He looked frail as he walked onto the ESPY stage and approached the microphone.

I thought to myself at that time, how would you live your life if you knew your days were numbered. If you knew death was imminent and you were about to pass to the other side, what kind of changes would you make in your life. How would you live every day? I suddenly felt like I had better pay attention to what this man had to say. So I grabbed a pen and a note pad and prepared to take notes.

Midway through his speech he made fun of the ESPN guy motioning to him that his speaking time was limited. Jim let him and everyone know that he was going to speak as long as he wanted. He said there are three things you need to do every day. If you do these three things every day, you are really living. First thing you must do every day is to laugh. I penned the notation. You should laugh every day. Second thing he said was that everyone should think. He said you need to spend a little time every day just in thought. And then, the third and last thing you need to do every day was to have your emotions moved to tears.

As I wrote these things down, I thought to myself. First laugh, I love to laugh. I can definitely laugh every day. Second, think. Yes, I am sure this is important. The day can get away from you. The week or the month can pass by so fast. Spend a little time everyday in thought, being thankful, reflect, plan, etc. This was great advice. And then the third thing, have your emotions moved to tears. Cry. Cry? How the heck am I going to do that? Cry? I cry maybe once a year. How is it possible to cry everyday and why would I want to?

20 years later, I still remember that brief sermon as if it were yesterday. It has stayed with me for 20 years and I am just now beginning to understand it. Sometimes an event in your life will help you see things from a different perspective, even change you. For me, the change has been due to raising two kids with special needs and culminating with the pregnancy and birth of our child with Down Syndrome. The result is that I am now touched by events I never paid attention to before.

An older brother caring for his little sister, a little service rendered by a neighbor, or the sweetness of holding a child in my arms can easily cause my eyes to water. Even the video from that person you had to move to your junk email because you could not handle another pass-along email, causes me to gush.

Sometimes you can hear a message and it will stay with you for years, all the while you do not know what it means. You may hear the same lesson 1000 times and not understand it. It is hard to define, but there is a process or event, which can prepare you to recognize and even possesses the full meaning. I mean really receive and internalize as if a new light has gone on. In my case it was a completely new sense. I can see, hear, touch, smell, and now my heart aches when I see sorrow and it leaps when I see happiness.

Not like before. Oh no. It's like a new dimension. I can have my emotions moved to tears, and I can do it every day. From that man, Coach Valvano, whose days were limited, I realized the importance of living each day to the fullest. Literally breathing his last words 20 years ago, and I finally get it. Every day I laugh. Every day I think. And every day I am moved to tears. Thank you Jimmy V! I get it now.

The Hurdles

"Let me tell you something you already know. The world ain't all sunshine and rainbows. It's a very mean and nasty place, and I don't care how tough you are, it will beat you to your knees and keep you there permanently if you let it. You, me, or nobody is gonna hit as hard as life. But it ain't about how hard you hit. It's about how hard you can get hit and keep moving forward; how much you can take and keep moving forward. That's how winning is done! Now, if you know what you're worth, then go out and get what you're worth. But you gotta be willing to take the hits, and not pointing fingers saying you ain't where you wanna be because of him, or her, or anybody. Cowards do that and that ain't you. You're better than that!" Rocky, Rocky Balboa

I used to wonder why life had dealt me different kids. In the dictionary, the word difference is followed by the word difficult. The two can be synonymous in your life. There is extra work with different. There are more challenges with different. Because of a different kid, your whole world is different. Difference is also synonymous with divergent and independent. Other options can include, if you are so inclined, delightful, awe-inspiring, amazing, and freaken awesome!

This is the moment when you decide what having a different child will be for you. You will be beat down. But can you take the hits and keep moving forward? Can you move forward without pointing fingers or looking for a short cut or way out? Do you realize your life has taken an opportunistic turn? Are you optimistic for the future? You may have trouble at times seeing the wonders ahead of you. But rest assured, your future is bright and far better than the one you imagine.

Different is the same as delightful, awe-inspiring, amazing, and freaken awesome! You won't accept separation, ignorance, or inactivity with your family. That's not you! You are not a coward! You will captain with your wife and right the ship when it lists to one side. You believe in giving support, guidance, and accepting new beginnings. **Failure is not an option**! Your family is too special, too valuable, and there is a good reason you are at the head of it.

When I was a junior in high school, I went out for track. The coach looked at me and said, "Daynes, we need you to run the hurdles." So I went over to the hurdles and spent the afternoon getting to know them. Do you know what I found out? I discovered I did not like them and they did not like me. I thought, no wonder he wants me to run the hurdles, because nobody else wants to. The hurdles stink! They are awkward, unnatural, you can fall hard, and they are difficult.

The next day I begrudgingly went out again to the hurdles and started to take notes from the few who had been doing it awhile. I started to run a little faster, consequently I fell a little harder. I focused more on my technique and less on my speed and I actually got faster. My battle with the hurdles continued as they persisted in slapping me around. There are ten of them all lined up in my lane staring me down. Inevitably one of them is going to take a shot at tripping me, and so I fell.

However, every day I ran through the hurdles, I got a little better. I worked on my awkward form and stopped jumping over the hurdles and started gliding through them. As the days passed, I noticed my technique getting better and my legs getting stronger. When I noticed my improvement, it served as motivation to keep going. There were more falls and last place finishes, but I could not help notice I was enjoying the hurdles!

I was different because I ran the hurdles and liked it. I enjoyed feeling and seeing progression in myself. What was once a total drag had become something I loved and looked forward to everyday. I now owned the hurdles. I was confident, stronger, faster, and ran with technique. That was reward enough, but I actually started winning!

What you have been given, is an obstacle. That's all. And obstacles are meant to be hurdled. Like many events in your life, it might be awkward and difficult when you begin hurdling these barriers. When you are dealing with change, it can be foreign and uncomfortable. You tire easily because your body is not yet in shape for it.

Those around you are in the same boat and they are tired of you. Have courage my friend, you will get over that hurdle.

You may be yelled at, nagged, lose your privileges, and get knocked down by hurdles in your lane, but as you work on your form, you will discover that you can glide through those hurdles. Take the notes within this work, and practice. Don't sell yourself short. Be confident. If you take these hurdles and manage them correctly, you will be a stronger and far better man than you were before.

You figure out how to turn lemons into lemonade. With each challenge surmounted, the lemonade gets sweeter and sweeter. Your breaking point, which felt so close, will become nothing but a distant memory. Falls will be less frequent and you will be quick to recover. The more you work on your form, the shorter your hurdles become. Gone are the fear, pride, and resentment. Those things weigh too much to be carried over the hurdles, so you shed them. You are the hurdler, moving forward, gliding through the obstacles, and striding in rhythm.

You probably did not ask for this obstacle. You did not want it, but it happened anyway. And now it is awesome, a game changer, even a life changer. This game will slow down for you, as you rise above and become adept to your new circumstances. See and feel the progression you achieve and thrive off of it. Hone in on your super powers, become the hurdler, become the man!

I used to wonder why life had dealt me different kids. Now I wonder how the heck I got so lucky as to hit the jackpot! Being able to laugh, think, and have your emotions moved to tears everyday is a small part of your new super powers. These powers are shared by Club members everywhere. It is part of our makeup. It is who we have become. It happened, not because of what you have been dealt, but how you dealt with it. You are here, you are winning, and you would not have it any other way.

Keep it together man!

Epilogue

KEEPITTOGETHERMAN.ORG

My goal in writing this book was to tell every man what they need to know about raising a special kid. I must admit however, there are deficiencies in this book. For example, the absence of a Special Needs Trust section is regrettable. This is something that many kids, including my own, need. It is of the utmost importance, yet, I did not write about it. At the moment changes are being made and I am trying to get the cost below $3500. We spend too much money on so many things related to special needs. I could not tell you to run out and drop that kind of dough.

It is our mission to bring the costs down, services up, empower couples, and strengthen families. The world of special needs is always evolving and changing. And so we learn and evolve with it. In our efforts to keep you updated on everything a dad needs to know from POG's to video editing to 'Things' to, well everything inside and out of this book, please visit keepittogetherman.org. It is a cornucopia of ideas, benes, resources, awards, and supports, to help you 'Keep It Together Man!'

End Notes

Introduction paragraph 5 page 7

1. 1 in 246 births: http://www.divinecaroline.com/22321/79258-probably-won-t-happen-putting-odds.

Phase 2 Acceptance; paragraph 1, page 60

2. National Institute of Mental Health: http://www.nimh.nih.gov/health/statistics/prevalence/any-disorder-among-children.shtml

Screen Sitters paragraph 8 page 72

3. http://makinghealtheasier.org/getmoving.

83% paragraph 1 page 103

4. http://www.friendshipcircle.org/blog/2010/11/03/80-divorce-rate-f.or-parents-with-a-child-who-has-autism/

Language Lessons paragraph 11 page 144

5. http://communitytable.parade.com/47689/emilylistfield/24-men-women-stress/.

Airplane 1st paragraph page 147

6. http://airodyssey.net/reference/inflight/

Contact Rick Daynes: info@keepittogetherman.org

Works Cited

Attwood, T. (1998). Asperger's Syndrome: A guide for Parents and Professionals. Philadelphia, PA: Jessica Kingsley Publishing.

Baker, B., Brightman, A. J., Heifetz,L. J., & Murphy, D. M. (1976). Behavior Problems. Champaign, IL: Research Press.

Beck, M. (1999). Expecting Adam. New York: Berkley Books.

Bortfeld, Holly. (2008, Oct.). GFCFSF Diet on a Budget - Talk About Curing Autism (TACA). Talk About Curing Autism (TACA). http://www.tacanow.org/family-resources/gfcfsf-diet-on-a-budget

California Special Education. (2008). California Special Education Programs: A Composite of Laws: Education Code - Part 30, Other Related Laws, and California Code of Regulations - Title 5. Sacramento, CA: California Department of Education

Canfield, C., Hansen, M. V., McNamara, H., & Simmons, K. (2007). Chicken Soup for the Soul: Children with Special Needs. Deerfield Beach, FL. Health Communications, Inc.

Eyre, R. & Eyre L. (2011). The Entitlement Trap: How to Rescue Your Child with a New Family System of Choosing, Earning, and Ownership. New York: Penguin Group.

Ferguson, D. & Parsons L. M.S. (2011). (dis)Abilities and the Gospel: How to Bring People with Special Needs Closer to Christ. Springville, UT: Cedar Fort Inc.

Gill, B. (1997) Changed By a Child: Companion Notes For Parents of a Child With a Disability. New York: Broadway Books.

Grandin, T. (2016). An Inside view of Autism. Autism Research Institute. http://www.autism.com/advocacy_grandin

Grandin, T. (2005). My experiences with visual thinking sensory problems and communication difficulties. Center for the Study of Autism. http ://www.autism.org/temple/visual.html

Grandin, T. (2005). Teaching tips for children and adults with autism. Center for the Study of Autism. http ://www.autism.org/ temple/tips.html

Haddon, M. (2003). The Curious Incident of the Dog in the Night-time. New York: Doubleday.

Ingersoll, B. & Dvortcsak, A. (2008) Teaching Your Child with ASD: Parents Guide. New York: Guilford Publications , Inc.

Kranowitz, C. S. (2005). The Out-of-sync Child: Recognizing and Coping with Sensory Processing Disorder. New York: Skylight Book/A Perigee Book.

Kurcinka, M. S. (2015). Raising Your Spirited Child: A Guide for Parents Whose Child Is More Intense, Sensitive, Perceptive, Persistent, and Energetic. New York, NY: William Morrow.

Kvols, K. (2006). Redirecting Children's Behavior. Gainesville, FL: International Network for Children and Families.

Latham, G. I. (2002). Christlike Parenting: Taking The Pain Out of Parenting. Seattle, WA: Gold Leaf Press

Lynn, G.T. M.A., M.P.A., L.M.H.C. with Lynn J.B. (2007) The Asperger Plus Child: How to   Identify and Help Children with Asperger Syndrome and Seven Common Co-existing Conditions. Shawnee Mission, Kansas: Autism Asperger Publishing Co.

McCarthy, J. (2007). Louder than Words: A Mother's Journey in Healing Autism. New York: Dutton.

McCarthy, J. (2008). Mother Warriors: A Nation of Parents Healing Autism against All Odds. New York: Dutton.

National Information Center for Children and Youth with Disabilities. (2002, October) A Parent's Guide: Communicating with your Child's School through letter writing. Washington, DC: NICHCY

National Institute of Mental Health. (2004, April). Autism spectrum disorders. Information Pamphlet, NIH Publications No. 04-5511. http://www.nih.gov

Schlessinger, L. (2004). The Proper Care & Feeding of Husbands. New York: Harper Collins Publishers.

Schlessinger, L. (2007). The Proper Care & Feeding of Marriage. New York: Harper Collins Publishers.

The Sensory Processing Disorder Network. (2008, September). Sensory Diet. SPD Network. http://www.spdnetwork.org/index.html

Silverstein, R. A. (2005) User's guide to the 2004 IDEA reauthorization. Consortium for Citizens with Disabilities. www.c-c-d.org

Skallerup, S. J. (2008). Babies with Down Syndrome: A New Parents' Guide. Bethesda, MD: Woodbine House.

Soper, K.L. (2007). Gifts: Mothers Reflect on How Children with Down Syndrome Enrich Their Lives. Bethesda, MD: Woodbine House

Wilens, T. (1999). Straight talk about psychiatric medications for kids. New York: Guilford.